MATTHEW

FINDING TREASURE NEW AND OLD

Mark Love

STREAMS of MERCY

study series

Matthew: Finding Treasure New and Old

HillCrest
PUBLISHING

1648 Campus Ct.
Abilene, TX 79601
www.hillcrestpublishing.com

Cover Design and Typesetting by Sarah Bales

Mark Love

Printed in the United States of America

ISBN 0-89112-235-4

1,2,3

Dedicated to my beloved wife Nancy,

my devoted partner

in discovering the way of mercy.

Recognizing the loving support of the

East County Church of Christ who learned

from Jesus the power of binding and loosing.

TABLE OF CONTENTS

FOR TEACHERS AND CLASS LEADERS...

The word of God is powerful. This belief is the driving force behind the Streams of Mercy Study Series. Assigned reading, brief commentary, and questions for reflection and class discussion are presented for each section of the biblical book. The goal is changed lives–changed by the power of the Word.

Consider the following suggestions as you prepare for class:

- Even though class members may have read the passage assigned for the week, select some verses to be read aloud in class: let the Word speak.

- Give a brief summary of the points made in the lesson, then begin working with the questions. As you prepare for your class, explore the possibility of a variety of answers to the questions. Don't be afraid of momentary silence when you ask the questions; give people a chance to think, but be prepared to prompt the discussion.

- Be creative with your classroom time. Sometimes have the class work in small groups to discuss the questions. Consider having someone prepare to comment on a particular question for the next scheduled class meeting. Perhaps, you could ask someone to be prepared to share his or her experience with finding time to work on the lesson in the middle of work and family obligations–in this way we acknowledge the struggle to make time for Bible study. Give someone the task of praying for the whole class throughout the coming week as they all find time for study. Let the class know this will be happening.

- Ask class members to make a plan of action that puts into practice the things the text calls for. This may be a service project or a commitment to pray for help in overcoming specific problems the text brings to light. Be prepared to suggest plans of action and to get the class involved in brainstorming about this. Avoid taking charge too much, let the class get involved.

- Find out if anyone in the class would like to create banners or any kind of visuals pertaining to the study. This is a good way to validate the gifts of others.

- Try to inspire excitement about the class working together each week to hear and understand the word of God. Stress that this is one of the ways we are in fellowship with one another.

- Be sensitive to people who don't want to speak in class. Encourage those who want to speak, but who may be a little tentative. Practice good leadership by not allowing any one person to dominate the discussions.

- Try to keep the discussions on target. One complaint we often hear about Bible classes is that the group too easily gets off the subject. These volumes are designed to promote discussion of the biblical text. Pray for help to keep the class focused without preventing healthy discussion.

Nothing is more important than seeking God's guidance as you prepare for class. Ask him to open your heart so the text speaks to you and convicts you, then you will be more prepared to lead the group. May the Lord bless all of you as you seek his will, and may you know the ever flowing streams of his mercy.

The Editors

INTRODUCTION

The Gospel of Matthew provides a word of encouragement for churches in the midst of transition, whether they are experiencing that transition in the first or the twenty-first century. Churches in transition ask the question, how do traditional ways of doing things make sense in the light of new circumstances? Questions of this nature can be very unsettling, especially when they involve ultimate issues like a community's relationship to God. The story of Jesus as told in Matthew persistently whispers reassuring words to those who find themselves in the shifting sands of change. "I am with you always," Jesus promises, "even to the end of the age."

These words would especially find their mark with Jewish Christians living in the aftermath of the destruction of the temple in Jerusalem by the Romans in 70 AD. Transitions often occur in the pivot points of time formed by cataclysmic events. For Jews living in Palestine, the world would never be the same. Before 70 AD the various Jewish "parties" – Sadducees, Pharisees, Zealots, and Essenes – were held together loosely by the chords of temple, land, and law. After the destruction of the temple, only the law remained to form the center of Jewish religious life. The interests of the Pharisees, centered in observing ritual aspects of the law and encompassing areas such as diet, sabbath observance, marriage laws, and tithing, were suited best for preserving and maintaining Jewish life apart from the temple. No longer were temple and priest the heart of religious life. Instead, the law and its interpreters, scribes or rabbis, took center stage. Synagogues, as places where the law was read and interpreted, became the authoritative centers of religious teaching and practice.

We often forget that Jewish Christians in Palestine continued in the practices of temple and synagogue even after the events of Pentecost (cf. Acts 2:46). Likely, these Christians saw themselves less as members of a new religious movement, and more as Jews who followed the teachings of Jesus Messiah. Undoubtedly, their confession of Jesus as messiah made them conscious of differences between themselves and other Jewish groups. Still, they likely continued to worship in the temple, observe sabbath restrictions, keep the Passover, and study the Scriptures in synagogues.

All of this changed dramatically after the destruction of the temple. In an effort to maintain identity, Jewish leaders circled the wagons to make sure that a visible and distinctive people would emerge from the rubble of Jerusalem's devastation. In closing the circle, followers of Jesus Messiah who actively pursued the making of Gentile converts were cut loose from the folds of the mother faith. These life-long Jews were excommunicated from synagogues and separated from the important ties of family, clan, and tribe. When Jesus warns the disciples in Matthew 10 that he is sending them out as sheep in the midst of wolves, Matthew's first readers undoubtedly saw themselves. When Jesus predicts that his followers will be handed over to sanhedrins and flogged in "their synagogues," Matthew's community likely shook their heads knowingly. They knew all too well that Jesus came not to bring peace, but a sword that would divide families and call for radical new allegiances (10:16-42). Ready or not, the first readers of Matthew's gospel had to imagine a life apart from the typical rhythms of their Jewish heritage. Separated from the synagogue, these Christians were becoming a church.

The first readers of Matthew's gospel were asking the hard questions of transition. Who exercises authority in these new circumstances? How will leaders be identified? What is the relationship between Jesus and the law? How should the law be interpreted? How are we to think of our neighbors, both Jew and Gentile? Is God with us in these new circumstances? In Matthew's gospel, the words of Jesus continue to speak in the shifting sands of transition. "I am with you, always, to the end of the age."

Matthew's Pastoral Artistry

Matthew's gospel was not just written to set the record straight. The author of Matthew writes to encourage churches to look again to Jesus for answers to their congregational problems. He writes with the heart of a pastor, choosing from the stories about Jesus those that best allow the Lord to speak again to his church. He writes with the passion of an artist, taking care at every turn to paint a compelling picture of Jesus. While Matthew is the first book in our New Testament, most believe it was not the first gospel written. Matthew appears not only to know of Mark's gospel, but also uses it as a primary source for the writing of his own. Matthew shares common stories with Luke, likely derived from collections of teachings of Jesus that the early Christians preserved over time. Some of the stories in Matthew are unique to his gospel and carry themes and motifs important to the gospel's pastoral intentions. By paying particular attention to how Matthew shapes and utilizes his sources to form a story, we learn something of his purpose in writing. By noticing hints and clues scattered throughout the gospel in literary devices like foreshadowing, repetition, or in devices like summaries, and insights into the thoughts of characters, readers will detect the author's footprints leading to true understandings of Jesus' life and ministry.

The picture Matthew paints of Jesus is indeed compelling. He is the Son of God, Israel's messiah. He is the fulfillment of all God's promises to Israel, the Davidic king, the true prophet of Israel, and the one who fulfills the demands of the law. He stands as one greater than Moses, eclipsing him and taking his place as Israel's true and authoritative teacher of righteousness. Jesus lives and proclaims the new and emerging realities of God's kingdom, making it on earth as it is in heaven. He calls his followers to a demanding righteousness in keeping with the realities of the kingdom. Yet, his yoke is easy and his burden is light because he understands that behind the law stands a God full of mercy. Unlike the scribes and Pharisees, Jesus is a reliable guide to knowing God because he knows the priority of mercy over sacrifice. He sends his followers into the world to make disciples of all nations. Yet, he does not send them alone. Jesus is Emmanuel, the continuing presence of God with his people.

For churches in transition, Jesus holds together both old and new realities. Every scribe trained for the kingdom of heaven will value old realities, understanding that

Jesus did not come to abolish the old way, but to fulfill it. However, kingdom scribes will also value new possibilities as Jesus pulls the church deeper into the heart of God. As I write this study guide, there is no plainer fact than that our churches are in the midst of profound transition. We live in a pivot point of history. We are invited with Matthew's first readers to build our house on the rock of knowing Jesus. This house will be adorned with treasures old and treasures new.

1
THEY SHALL NAME HIM EMMANUEL

MATTHEW 1:1-2:23

HUNGER AND THIRST

I have this fantasy, common among ministers perhaps, that all the New Testament writers have assembled at the Downtown Hilton for consultation. I take my place in line with all the other hopeful ministers–a line like a teller line at the bank. Once you get to the front you wait for the next available teller. I am counting places in line, trying to anticipate which NT writer will give me an audience. I'm hoping for Paul. His experience with a variety of churches will be of tremendous value to me. I serve a church in the hard throes of transition. Pressures without and changes within often make ministry in my congregation a perilous enterprise. How can I reassure my congregation that God is with us in the midst of the change that characterizes transition?

Finally, I am to the front of the line. The next available writer is Matthew. I can't help the feeling of disappointment. How will he be able to help? He gives me an autographed first edition of his gospel; I smile weakly. "Why the long face?" he asks. "No offense," I reply, "but I've got church trouble. I need advice, not stories." I relate to him my transition predicament. "Sounds familiar," he says nodding knowingly. "That's why I wrote this gospel. Talk about a church in a perilous transition! Separating from the synagogue brought excommunication, divided families, and a host of new issues related to what it meant to be a church. We were in uncharted waters. How do you know God is with you in dangerous waters?" "Exactly!" I exclaimed. He leaned back. "Let me tell you a story. I think it speaks to your situation. The birth of Jesus the Messiah happened in this way..."

HEARING THE STORY

We encounter stories with our imaginations, not so much with magnifying glass and highlighter pen. We experience before we dissect. Read the story aloud in your group (choose an expressive reader, preferably one who has rehearsed the story). Let the dramatic movement of the narrative form impressions. Welcome the characters as they are introduced. Allow your heart to form allegiances. Allow the emotion, pace, cadence, and description of the scenes to form impressions.

1. What impressions did the characters leave? Describe the roles of Joseph, Herod, and the Wise Men. How does the angel of the Lord help you interpret the story? Where does the narrator interject his viewpoints?

2. What words or phrases repeat or take center stage?

WHAT WILL JOSEPH DO?

This story begins perilously. While the coming of God's Messiah should bring joy and triumph, the opening chapters of Matthew are draped with fear and anxiety. The fear of Joseph and Herod give the story energy and draw the attention of the reader. Joseph's fear, or anxiety, is related to Mary's being with child before their marriage. Joseph is "betrothed" to Mary, a legal arrangement that preceded the actual marriage of the participants. While Mary "belonged" to Joseph during the period of betrothal, she lived with her family until the time of the wedding. Mary's pregnancy during the period of betrothal was cause for scandal. What will Joseph do? Will he divorce Mary or take her as his wife?

The text describes Joseph as a righteous man. This designation is supremely important in Matthew. Jesus calls his followers to a righteousness that exceeds that of the scribes and Pharisees (5:21). What does it mean here for Joseph to be a righteous man in the context of Mary's pregnancy? Jewish law not only allowed for a divorce in situations like this, it demanded it. According to the law, a woman committing adultery became unclean to her husband, or in this case to her betrothed (Deut. 24:1-4, cf. 22:13-30). To those who know the law, Joseph's decision to "divorce her quietly" demonstrates a concern for righteousness. Beyond Joseph's obligation to the law, however, lie other motivations. Joseph not only chooses to divorce Mary, but to do it quietly in a way that won't expose her to shame. This is no small consideration. In Joseph's world, notions of honor and shame defined identities and marked the boundaries of social movement. A man's ability to participate in the public world depended upon his honor standing. In contrast, women lived in the private sphere to uphold the honor of their husbands by not bringing shame to the family. Mary's pregnancy places Joseph's honor at risk. Joseph's merciful decision not to shame Mary might well have been a decision to lose honor in the eyes of others. From Matthew's perspective, Joseph is righteous for two reasons: he is concerned to uphold the law, and he demonstrates a concern for mercy, which is the heart of the law.

What the reader knows that Joseph doesn't is that God is behind Mary's being found with child. She is with child from the Holy Spirit. By putting Mary away, Joseph would be turning his back on the Messiah of God. Yet, to embrace Mary and the child would be to walk into the public disgrace of their awkward circumstance. Joseph's ultimate decision to take Mary as his wife is likely a decision to bear her shame. The implication of his decision for observers would be either that he acted improperly toward her during the time of betrothal or that he disregarded the demands of the law. Though a righteous man, Joseph needs to be oriented to God's work behind the scenes, so that he might choose an even more righteous path. This righteous path is not limited to letters on a page, but is rooted in the character of a merciful God. Mercy is rarely routine and often upsets our equilibrium. The entry of God's Messiah into the world is by necessity a scandal, a departure from business as usual, and Joseph needs to be invited into the scandal.

Mercy is rarely routine and often upsets our equilibrium.

The story moves from peril to safety through a series of dreams in which the angel of the Lord teaches Joseph the will of God. "Do not be *afraid*," the angel says, "to take Mary as your wife" (1:20). To those who know Scripture, the angel's words have a reassuring familiarity. The birth of a special son in the Old Testament is often announced by a heavenly messenger who gives the designation of a name along with a destiny for the child (cf. Ishmael, Gen 16:11-12; Isaac, Gen 17:19; Solomon, 1 Chr 22:9-10). We are on familiar soil here—soil upon which God acts for his people. In this instance, the child is to be named Jesus (God saves), "for he will save his people from their sins" (1:21). Those whom Jesus saves will call him "Emmanuel" – "God with us." Though the circumstances of Joseph's life appear scandalous, they are nothing less than evidence of the presence of God. Joseph, a righteous man, hears what the angel says and acts on it. "When Joseph awoke from his sleep, he did as the angel of the Lord commanded him." This is what it means to be a disciple in Matthew.

⁂ Reflection and Application

1. Even before the birth of Jesus, Joseph models what it means to be a disciple, or righteous man. How would you define discipleship from the example of Joseph in this story?

2. What is Joseph's relationship to the law? What is it that allows him to move beyond the law to a higher righteousness?

THE THREAT OF HEROD

The story moves from Joseph's inner turmoil over Mary's pregnancy to the outward threat posed by Herod. Herod was appointed "King of the Jews" by the Romans in 40 BCE. He died in 4 BCE. An able politician, he was known for his massive building projects and for cruelty toward his own family. It would not be difficult for the reader to cast Herod in the role of villain.

Herod's interest in Jesus is contrasted with the interest of the Magi. The Magi are looking for the one "who is born king of the Jews. For we have seen his star at its rising and have come to pay homage to him" (2:2). They appear here as astronomers/astrologers who chart the heavens to look for evidence of significant historical events. While they find in the stars cause for homage and celebration, Herod finds the threatening report of a rival king. The child will be king of the Jews, and not by the fiat of the Romans, but by virtue of his lineage. Herod, like Joseph, was "frightened" (2:3), and his fear places the story at risk.

Again, the story is saved by the intervention of God through dreams. The Magi are warned in a dream of Herod's plan to destroy the child. Joseph is warned in a dream of Herod's intent to destroy the child and is told to flee to Egypt. This spares the child from Herod's order to have all the male infants in and around Bethlehem killed. Upon Herod's death, Joseph is told in a dream to return with his family to "Israel" and further warned not to settle near Bethlehem, but in Galillee. God is clearly "with Joseph" in this perilous beginning. Emmanuel!

ᕯ Reflection and Application

1. How are the circumstances of Mary and Joseph's life similar to the circumstances of Matthew's church (see introduction)? Why would they need to hear a story about "God with us"?

2. Why would a story be an effective way to make the point "God with us" to a struggling church? How does a story function in ways different than a letter or epistle? What advantages does a story possess?

ALL THIS TOOK PLACE TO FULFILL...

We learn much about the identity of Jesus from Matthew's infancy narrative. Conceived by the Spirit of God, he is Son of God. Born in Bethlehem, he is Son of David, King of the Jews, God's anointed one, or Messiah. He is king, redeemer, savior, and shepherd. Some of these identifications are embedded in the details of the narrative, and some, Matthew takes pains to point out. The repeated refrain, "this took place to fulfill . . ." (1:22; 2:5; 2:15; 2:17; 2:23), establishes Jesus' identity as the culminating figure of Israel's history.

Matthew's use of Old Testament "fulfillment" passages elicits a great deal of interest among biblical scholars. We often think of fulfillment only in terms of the prediction of a prophecy. Many of the texts Matthew cites, however, are not predictive in any sense. In their original context, they seem to have nothing to do with the future life of God's messiah. But for Matthew, fulfillment does not always have to be traced back to a specific prediction. To Matthew, details of Jesus' life have the ring of God's story. "Isn't this just like God? Isn't this how he works? Haven't we seen God work this way before?" The story of Jesus follows traces already well cut and worn by the story of Israel. If we know the story of Israel, the details of Jesus' life are just what we would expect and they call certain passages to mind. In this more general sense, Jesus fulfills Scripture. As Harrington suggests, "The point is that Jesus' life from start to finish was in perfect harmony with the Scriptures. Or to put it more in keeping with Matthew's outlook—the Scriptures are in perfect harmony with Jesus' life."[1]

⁂ Reflection and Application

1. Matthew begins his gospel with a look at Jesus' family tree. Why would roots be important to Matthew's theme of fulfillment? Notice that the genealogy begins with Abraham and not with Adam (cf. Luke 3:23-38). Adam is every person's father. Whose father is Abraham? Does this give us any clues about Matthew's audience? Finally, what would it mean for Jesus to be descended from King David?

2. Why would the theme of fulfillment be so important to a church transitioning away from the synagogue?

A CLOSER LOOK

1. Joseph functions as a model disciple in these opening stories. He hears the word of God and is obedient. Is your spirit as willing and responsive as Joseph's? The way for Jesus is paved, in a sense, by his obedience. Is your life sufficiently obedient to the call of God to prepare the way for Jesus to be present in this world? Pray for an obedient spirit.

2. Is your story one of anxiety or fear? Matthew's gospel begins with an encouraging promise. God is with you even if circumstances seem to suggest otherwise. Live in the promise. Receive it as a gift from God. Welcome Emmanuel into your life. Give your burdens to him. List the ways you have seen, or hope to see, God present in the midst of your anxiety. Pray for eyes to discern his presence.

---

[1] Daniel Harrington, *The Gospel of Matthew*, Sacra Pagina Commentaries, (Collegeville, MN: The Liturgical Press, 1991), 17.

2
"UNLESS YOUR RIGHTEOUSNESS EXCEEDS..."

MATTHEW 5:1-48

HUNGER AND THIRST

We all know the old saw, "laws are made to be broken." This saying may be offered as a comment on the limited adequacy of laws. We all know stories of enforcement of the "letter of the law" that betrays the spirit of the law. Jesus knew the same thing. Later we will see him take the Pharisees to task for keeping the letter of the law so that they can avoid "weightier matters" (23:23-24). This kind of law keeping brings the sternest rebuke in Matthew's gospel – "hypocrite!"

Yet, we will see in this unit that law, or Torah, is an important category for Jesus and for Matthew's church. The question of proper observance of the law would be foremost in the minds of those living in the transition from synagogue to church. The Christians in Matthew's church always imagined their life before God in relation to the Torah. They were concerned with the demands and limits of the law and discussed and debated how to bind and loose (see **A Closer Look** below) in relation to the law. What does it mean to honor the law now as a Christian?

The Oregon Driver's Handbook is not a scintillating read. As I read sterile language of Oregon traffic law I do not imagine an author who is trying to communicate to me something of himself and what he deems important. I see no faces. But Torah is not this way. In reading God's law we are to see his face. This is a concern of Matthew's gospel. How does one read the law so as to see clearly the face of God? This quest leads to a higher righteousness.

HEARING THE STORY

The Sermon on the Mount forms the first of five teaching discourses in Matthew (5:1-7:28; 10:1-11:1; 13:1-53; 18:1-19:1; 23:1-26:1). These five discourses are connected by the concluding phrase, "when Jesus had finished saying these things... ." Moreover, they seem to be arranged in corresponding parts as follows:

A1 Sermon on the Mount   B1 Mission discourse
                     C Kingdom parables
B2 Community discourse   A2 Woes, Coming of the Kingdom

This arrangement is called a *chiasm* (from the Greek letter *chi* which looks like an "X") and will become more evident as we study each of the discourses. For now notice two things. First, there are five discourses. What significance might that have for Matthew's audience? Second, notice that the Beatitudes (5:1-11) which begin the Sermon on the Mount have corresponding woes at the beginning of the final discourse (23:1-36).

I have divided this magnificent sermon into two studies. Chapter 5, the focus of this lesson, is critical to understanding all of Jesus' teaching in Matthew. Fundamental principles for interpreting life in the emerging kingdom are laid out here. Chapter 5:13-20 is the strategic center and provides clues for understanding the rest of the sermon. As a group you may want to read aloud the entire sermon to hear how it unfolds as a whole. Pay particular attention to how this first chapter revolves around verses 13-20.

✤ Reflection and Application

1. What important principles are related in verses 13-20? Why would these verses be pivotal to understanding the rest of the chapter? The rest of the sermon?

2. Many suggest that Jesus' teaching from a mountain invites necessary comparisons with Moses. We already noticed that there are five discourses in Matthew. Could this be a parallel to the five books of Moses (Genesis-Deuteronomy)? Are there parallels to the story of Moses in Matthew's infancy narrative? What conclusions might you draw concerning the relationship of Jesus to Moses?

UNLESS YOUR RIGHTEOUSNESS EXCEEDS...

Jesus as teacher of God's right-eousness is call-ing a renewed Israel to a demanding way of living.

Verses 13-20 orient Matthew's readers to both the ministry of Jesus and the community that follows his teaching. While many Old Testament images and traditions lie behind these important verses, pictures from Isaiah might best give insight into Matthew's meaning. Isaiah 2:2ff looks forward to a day when the Lord's house will be established as the highest mountain and become a place where the nations gather to hear instruction from the Lord. God's people are called to "walk in the light of the Lord" (2:5). These images are picked up again in chapter 42 and 49 as the Servant of the Lord gathers Israel again to make them a light to the nations (42:6; 49:6). In the Sermon on the Mount, Jesus brings instructions from the Lord that will create a true Israel. This community will in turn be light and salt among the nations.

Jesus is the authoritative teacher of Israel. To a community wondering about their relationship to God's law, Jesus states emphatically that he has come not to abolish the law and prophets, but to fulfill them. Matthew's community learns from Jesus that their separation from the synagogue is not a separation from the teachings of Israel, but rather a move deeper into the heart of these teachings. This deeper move comes through a desire to teach and perform Torah. Those who are least in God's kingdom are those who break commands and teach others to do the same. Conversely, those great in the kingdom teach and live Torah. Jesus is confident those who follow his program of Torah observance will shine as a light because their righteousness will exceed that of the scribes and Pharisees. Jesus as teacher of God's righteousness is calling a renewed Israel to a demanding way of living.

❧ Reflection and Application

1. In the phrase "you are the light of the world," "you" is plural, not singular. Is this an important distinction? Why would God have a preference for forming communities, not just individuals?

2. The "law and the prophets" is often Hebrew shorthand for the entire Old Testament. How important should the Old Testament be to Christians in Matthew's church? To our churches today?

YOU HAVE HEARD IT WAS SAID, BUT I SAY TO YOU...

Jesus came to fulfill the law and the prophets. Several important questions proceed from this claim. How does Jesus read Torah? What does it mean to be a law-keeper? 5:21-48 help answer these questions. They orient the reader to Jesus' program of Torah observance.

Nearly all rabbis in Jesus' day recognized the need to find the center of the law or to honor what was at the heart of God's will in giving the law. With a dynamic center, the law could continue to have voice and force in changing circumstances. For some this meant finding a few laws foundational to all other commands and delineating them in such detail that they would not be transgressed either intentionally or unintentionally. For example, by focusing on a strict and elaborate observance of things that made one clean or unclean, a person could be fairly certain not to transgress the purpose of the giving of the law, which was to create a holy people. This manner of Torah observance, attributed to the Pharisees in Matthew, carries the advantage of maintaining strict boundaries for defining insiders and outsiders. However, this approach carries the disadvantages of being superficial, divisive and legalistic.

Jesus moves in another direction. Instead of reducing the observance of Torah to a few well-defined areas of the law, he *expands* the notion of what it means to observe Torah. This expansive view is seen in the formula, "You have heard that it was said ..., but I say unto you..." Jesus does not abolish the command as he offers these contrast statements, but rather pushes the listener deeper into the implications of the command. For example, he recognizes that anger is the root of murder (5:22), and that lust is at the root of adultery (5:28). The law must be read to find the deeper principles and motivations that allow authentic righteousness to emerge in a person's life. Jesus understands that the letter is not the end of the law, a person is. He can expand the demands of the Torah not simply because he reads the law correctly, but because he reads God correctly. Torah observance should make the law-keeper like the law-giver. This is likely the meaning behind Jesus' exhortation, "Be perfect, therefore, as your heavenly Father is perfect" (5:48). Perfection in Matthew is not found in a superficial keeping of the rules, nor does it mean that God expects us to always do the right thing. The pursuit of perfection in Matthew involves becoming like God. The secret of fulfilling righteousness is not to limit one's observance of the law, but to push deeper into what it means to love God and neighbor, and in so doing to become more like God himself.

❧ Reflection and Application

> This is a demanding righteousness. No one in your group can claim complete compliance with the demands of Jesus. For instance, all in your group might be able to claim innocence with regard to murder, but would have to plead guilty to being angry with their brother at some point. Could this be the beginning of community? Who in your group can claim to be rabbi?

FOR THEIRS IS THE KINGDOM OF HEAVEN

How does Jesus read Torah? This is certainly an important question in Matthew's gospel. But it is not the first question answered by the Sermon on the Mount. The beatitudes answer the question, "what kind of *person* can teach *and* observe the law?" As the first word of this important section that defines Jesus' relation to the law and the prophets (5:1-48), Matthew reminds his church that faithful lives produce faithful readers. The poor in spirit, the meek, the merciful, and the peacemakers are those most likely to recognize the God who stands behind his Scripture.

As noted above, the beatitudes seem to correspond to the woes found in 23:1-36. The combination of blessings and woes form a recognizable literary form known as "ascription" (cf. Lk. 6:20-49). Matthew likely expects the reader to make this connection between the first and last teaching discourses. Parallel structure between the beatitudes and woes in Matthew reinforces this association. Both the first beatitude and woe deal with the kingdom of heaven (5:3; 23:13). Both the last beatitude and woe deal with the persecution of prophets (5:11-12; 23:29-36). Both the beatitudes and woes feature mercy in the middle saying (5:7; 23:23). There seems little doubt that these are corresponding texts.

This raises an interesting possibility. The woes begin with a warning against the scribes and Pharisees, "those who sit on Moses' seat," who do not practice what they teach (23:1-3). Jesus is concerned to find scribes who teach and practice the commandments of God (5:19-20). Could it be that the beatitudes provide a character description of a Christian scribe who stands in contrast to the Pharasaic scribe? Jesus' audience in the Sermon on the Mount seems to be two-tiered. While the crowds are present, the disciples form an inner circle and seem to be the primary focus of the teaching (5:1). In Matthew's gospel, the disciples often represent Christian teachers.

While the traits listed in the beatitudes apply to all who follow Jesus (the listening crowd), they are especially significant for those who teach.

Leadership is a crucial issue for a group in transition. Who can be trusted? Who can faithfully interpret Torah in this new situation? Who stands in continuity with Jesus? In the beatitudes, Matthew gives his church a character description for determining faithful leaders.

ᴥ Reflection and Application

1. Much has been written lately on the subject of how to read and interpret the Bible (hermeneutics). The "how" of Bible study is certainly important. How important is the "who" of Bible study? How would the character traits listed in the beatitudes make you a better interpreter of Scripture?

2. This section has suggested that the beatitudes might provide a character description for Christian teachers/leaders in Matthew's community. Think about the qualities listed for elders in the pastoral epistles (1 Tim 3:1-7; Titus 1:5-9). Do the beatitudes describe the same person? Could a person meet the "qualifications" of an elder in 1 Timothy and Titus and still not possess traits like "poor in spirit," or "peacemaker?" How might the beatitudes assist a church in identifying its leaders today?

3. Spend time praying over the beatitudes this week. They are not a cafeteria-style list from which we might pick and choose. They describe a whole life celebrated by the kingdom of God. Pray everyday this week with the beatitudes in front of you. Allow these words to call you into a deeper righteousness. You will be on your way to becoming more like God.

4. Jesus hopes to form a community that is salt and light in the world. Both are ruined by inconsistency. Jesus hopes to find people who will be great in the kingdom—who will teach and observe his teachings. We call this walking the talk. Choose to be light and salt this week through having a more consistent witness. Let your life match your confession.

A CLOSER LOOK

Jesus refers to binding and loosing in two very strategic texts in Matthew (16:19; 18:18-20). The sayings are unique to Matthew and may provide a valuable point of contrast between the synagogues and the emerging churches for whom the gospel is written. In Jewish communities, certain scribes carried the authority to bind and loose. Their duties appear to be two-fold. First, scribes interpreted the law and ruled on what was binding in particular circumstances. Second, they carried the authority to excommunicate (bind) or extend forgiveness (loose) on those who transgressed the standards of the community. Living apart from the influence of those who "sit on Moses' seat" (23:2), the emerging church needs clarification on how to live in relation to the law and to each other. Binding and loosing would be a practice crucial for the survival and function of Matthew's community. While the Sermon on the Mount never mentions the practice of binding and loosing, Jesus' teaching here establishes understandings crucial for this practice. Matthew 5:17-48 orients the church to Jesus' approach to interpreting the law. The beatitudes describe the character necessary to bind and loose in keeping with the values of the kingdom.

3
YOUR FATHER WHO IS IN SECRET...

MATTHEW 6:1-7:28

HUNGER AND THIRST

In his fable, "The Magic Eyes," Lewis Smedes describes a baker named Fouke as "a righteous man, with a long thin chin and a long thin nose. Fouke was so upright that he seemed to spray righteousness from his thin lips over everyone who came near him; so the people of Faken preferred to stay away."[1] Smedes' description points to a problem associated with any human attempt to be righteous. The line between holy and holier-than-thou is a thin one not easily negotiated. We all know people whose "righteousness" makes them unapproachable – whose lives seem to be above the rubble the rest of us know. Far from inviting us into their circle, they seem to repel us. Authentic community withers in the glare of their imposing uprightness.

Behind our aversion to those holier-than-thou lurks a suspicion that no one can be that good. We sense that their uprightness is a moral sleight-of-hand, an illusion sustained by smoke and mirrors. All too often, our suspicions are confirmed. Behind the facade of righteousness lie cracks and faults just like our own. Alas (or aha!), they are hypocrites.

How does a person or community avoid the charge of hypocrite? Lower our standards and live like everyone else? This is not an option for Jesus. As we noted in the previous lesson, Jesus calls his followers to a righteousness that exceeds that of the scribes and Pharisees. Jesus also, however, expects his people to be attractive, to be both salt and light. How can God's people aspire to a greater righteousness without spraying it over all who come near? This, it seems, is a narrow path and few there are who find it.

HEARING THE STORY

At first glance the latter parts of the Sermon on the Mount seem less structured than the opening sections. To this way of thinking, these chapters resemble the wisdom literature (e.g., Proverbs) in which short, loosely connected sayings form a collage to give a general impression of a wise or virtuous life. The parable of the wise and foolish builders at the end of the Sermon on the Mount (7:24-27), seems to fit this view. Typical of wisdom material, two paths are presented to those who listen to Jesus, one wise and the other foolish. Jesus sits atop the mountain as the true sage of Israel.

---

[1] Lewis Smedes, *Forgive and Forget: Healing the Hurts We Don't Deserve*, (New York: Harper & Row, 1984), 13.

While the wisdom themes of the latter sections of this sermon are undeniable, viewing these statements as loosely connected may obscure their contribution to earlier points in the sermon. As you read this portion of the sermon aloud, see how many associations you can make with the previous unit.

⁂ Reflection and Application

1. Try to notice markers in the text. What sayings seem to go together? Which begin with the same phrase or follow a similar literary formula? Locate summary statements. How would you group the sayings in this passage?

2. What themes have you noticed that run throughout the sermon?

PRACTICING YOUR RIGHTEOUSNESS (6:1-18)

Three acts of piety were considered central to being a religious person in Jesus' day: almsgiving, prayer, and fasting. In this section of the sermon, Jesus affirms traditional religious practices, but pushes his audience to look beyond the acts themselves and to consider the motivations that stand behind them. Again, Jesus is interested in a righteousness that exceeds that of the scribes and Pharisees. He is interested in a depth of righteousness that demonstrates a consistency of attitudes and actions.

For each act of piety considered, Jesus' instruction is contrasted with practices that are hypocritical. Namely, those who practice their faith to be seen by others are contrasted with those who practice in secret. The point is clear in each instance. Those who display their faith to be admired by others already have their reward, the praise of others. This disqualifies them from the reward given by God who "sees in secret." This is the fate of hypocrites.

Matthew uses the term hypocrite more than all of the rest of the books of the New Testament combined. The withering attack on scribes and Pharisees in the final discourse (23:1-36) resounds with charges of their being hypocrites and blind guides. These are people whose inner motives contradict their outward actions. While hypocrisy may take many forms, its religious varieties are particularly lethal and damnable. Rhoads points out "religion often becomes an insidious means to mask our hypocrisy, because we use the claim of sacredness as a shield against self-examination and criticism."[2]

In contrast to the way of the hypocrite which is public and elaborate, Jesus offers secrecy and simplicity as mechanisms for self-examination and criticism. For example, the model prayer Jesus offers his disciples is to be said in one's room with the door shut and is to be economical in expression – unlike the Gentiles who heap phrase upon

---

[2] David Rhoads, *The Challenge of Diversity: The Witness of Paul and the Gospels* (Minneapolis: Fortress Press), 87.

phrase. The Lord's Prayer contains no new words for prayer. Jewish prayers, like the Eighteen Benedictions, contain phrases and ideas present in Jesus' model prayer. What distinguishes the Lord's Prayer is its brevity and simplicity. Jesus' views on almsgiving, prayer, and fasting demonstrate an awareness that religion can become performance oriented. He asks his followers to turn from trusting in the performance of their religion, to trusting in God who sees what is done in secret.

❧ Reflection and Application

1. Why is it difficult to perform good deeds in secret? What rewards do we deny ourselves when we do things unnoticed? How might these rewards stand in the way of our truly trusting in God?

2. How is secrecy an antidote to hypocrisy? What traits or virtues would we have to develop to be content with a secret righteousness? Read the beatitudes again. Which traits in the beatitudes would make one more likely to be content with a secret righteousness?

3. If we don't do things to be seen by others, how can our religious life be considered the light of the world? Is this hiding our light under a bushel? Is there something brighter than a bumper sticker, a fish symbol on a car, or a t-shirt with John 3:16 emblazoned on it? By which light could the world better see God?

DO NOT BE ANXIOUS (6:19-7:12)

This section presents a variety of sayings dealing with diverse topics like wealth, light and darkness, judging, and prayer. Are they simply a potpourri? I would suggest that they are linked loosely by the themes of anxiousness and trust. This emphasis is undeniable in 6:19-34 where four times Jesus calls his followers to not be anxious (vv. 25, 28, 31, 34). The person who stores up treasures on earth is also the person who will be anxious about food, drink, and clothing. Instead of focusing upon these things, the child of God should seek first and exclusively the kingdom of God. The person who is anxious serves two masters, and it is impossible to serve both God and mammon. The one who seeks the kingdom of heaven possesses an eye full of light. This person sees the world from a healthy perspective and stands in contrast to the hypocrite who is a blind guide (23:13, 15, 16, 23, 25, 27, 29). The word "healthy" (6:22, NRSV) can literally be translated "simple," "single," or "undivided." Unlike the hypocrite who serves two masters, the non-anxious disciple has a singleness of vision and heart resulting in undivided loyalties and consistency in living.

This singleness of focus appears in 7:1-12 as well. The one seeking the kingdom of heaven is the one who asks, seeks, and knocks. This disciple knows the Father will provide (7:11). This attitude of trust spills over into relationships with others. God can be trusted with the business of judgement. A follower of Jesus needs to avoid the trap of the hypocrite who judges the speck in another's eye while a beam remains in his own. In a similar way, the one who trusts God to provide can live doing "to others as you would have them to do to you; for this is the law and the prophets" (7:12).

Underlying many of the sayings in this section is the principle of simplicity. The follower of Jesus does not gather treasures on earth. The follower of Jesus serves one master, pursues one agenda, and possesses a single or simple eye. The follower of Jesus understands the law and the prophets simply: to treat others as they would be treated. Again, simplicity is offered as an antidote to hypocrisy and a hedge against anxiety.

🌱 Reflection and Application

1. We live in a consumer driven world offering us a variety of choices. Our lives are increasingly complex and anxiety producing. Is this more than an issue of time management? Might there be an underlying spiritual problem associated with complex lives? Is complexity a step toward hypocrisy? Discuss how competing loyalties might lead to hypocrisy.

2. What would we gain spiritually by simplifying our lives? How would simplicity of life help one avoid the charge of being a hypocrite?

THE ROAD IS HARD THAT LEADS TO LIFE (7:13-27)

The Sermon on the Mount begins with blessings. It ends with warnings. The road is wide that leads to destruction. Beware of false prophets! Not everyone who says "Lord, Lord," will enter the kingdom of heaven. Take care that you are not a foolish man building on a shifting foundation! Why end with warnings?

I have suggested that Matthew was written for a church in transition. The beginning of the Sermon on the Mount erased familiar boundaries. "You have heard that it was said..., but I say to you... ." While the statements found in 7:13-27 provide warnings, they also set boundaries. Jesus is pushing the church into a new way of life that will require new skills of navigation. It is an expansive way calling for a demanding righteousness. It is nice to have a few "dangerous curves" signs when traveling new roads. To a church in transition, Jesus warns "take care which path you choose. Choose your leaders carefully. Don't be overly impressed with wonder workers. Choose character over charisma." Good advice for a group in transition.

Two final observations. First, the sermon ends with a familiar refrain. The wise man is the one who both hears *and* performs the commands of Jesus (7:24; cf. 5:19). Such a one is not a blind guide or a hypocrite. Second, the saying about the narrow gate and the hard way (7:14) needs to be heard in the overall context of Matthew's gospel. While the way of Jesus is a demanding yoke, it is also easy to bear (11:28-30). I would like to suggest that in the context of the Sermon on the Mount, the narrow

24

path is learning to be holy without being holier-than-thou. This is a way, we will see, marked by mercy

A CLOSER LOOK

1. The Lord's Prayer was said by early Christians three times daily. It is a prayer that teaches us how to pray at other times. Yet, we rarely say it. Try saying it every day for the next two weeks. Better, try saying it both morning and evening for the next two weeks.

2. Simplicity is a long-honored Christian discipline. Today, we live exceedingly complex lives that cry out for simplicity. Often, this complexity is related to our efforts to try to serve both God and Mammon. Could less be more? Pray this week that God will show you ways you need to simplify your life.

4
HE TOOK OUR INFIRMITIES AND BORE OUR DISEASES

MATTHEW 8:1-9:38

HUNGER AND THIRST

In the Sermon on the Mount Jesus calls his followers to a righteousness that exceeds that of the scribes and the Pharisees. He calls them to be perfect as God is perfect and to find the narrow path which is difficult to tread. Followers are called to practice their religion in secret, to radically trust God for their daily needs, to give to everyone who begs from them, and to turn the other cheek. This is a demanding way. Who would try it? A few brave of heart, inspired by the idealism of the kingdom, might try to live in this kingdom. The rest of us, all too aware of our feeble and fragile lives would be hesitant to attempt it. My sense is that we would need to trust the one leading us into this way of life. We would need not only to know he is powerful and authoritative, but also compassionate and responsive, for he calls us into a life with seemingly little margin for error. Who is this Jesus who calls us into a demanding righteousness?

HEARING THE TEXT

This section reveals the theological artistry of Matthew's gospel. It features three sets of three narratives (8:1-17; 8:23-9:8; 9:18-34) that display Jesus' authority to heal, control nature, cast out demons, and forgive sins. At the end of each set of narratives an evaluation is provided to help the reader clearly understand the meaning of Jesus' ministry (8:17; 9:8; 9:33-34). Matthew places a story about discipleship after the first and second set of narratives (8:18-22; 9:9-17). The writer wants us to understand discipleship, at least in part, in relation to these stories about Jesus' authority. The section ends with a summary of Jesus' ministry that functions as a transition into the teaching discourse that begins in 10:1. The transition helps us understand what precedes it and helps us anticipate what will follow. As you read this section aloud, allow the structure to provide clues to what the stories mean.

❧ Reflection and Application

1. How do the evaluations offered (8:17; 9:8; 9:33-34) help us understand the identity of Jesus? How does this correspond with what we have already seen about Jesus? What makes the last evaluation unique?

2. The two stories on discipleship (8:18-22; 9:9-17) occupy strategic ground. How do they correspond to the picture of Jesus provided in the other stories in this unit? Are the two stories created equal? What themes seem to be important in the second discipleship story?

HE BORE OUR DISEASES

In this section we see Jesus do amazing things. We also hear things said about him. Taken together, things both seen and heard, we discover that Jesus is both authoritative and compassionate. We noticed Matthew's emphasis on Jesus' authority at the end of the Sermon on the Mount, "he taught them as one having authority" (7:29). In this cycle of stories, we see his authority in the deeds he performs. He demonstrates power over disease, demons, and the elements. His works reveal the authority of the kingdom of heaven. To use a phrase from the model prayer, his ministry makes it on earth as it is in heaven. In this way, his healing authority is linked to his authority to forgive sins (9:2-8). What he forgives on earth is forgiven in heaven.

Now listen to what is said about Jesus. Matthew underlines this picture of authority with what is said in both the dialogues and statements of evaluation found within the stories (8:2-3; 8:8-9; 8:27; 9:8; 9:28; 9:33). Those who encounter Jesus recognize his authority by calling him "Lord" (8:2, 6, 25, 9:28). For instance, the centurion clearly recognizes Jesus' authority: "Lord, I am not worthy to have you come under my roof; but only say the word and my servant will be healed. For I am a man under authority, with soldiers under me ..." (8:8-9). The crowds see Jesus the way the centurion does: "When the crowds saw it, they were filled with awe and glorified God, *who had given such authority to human beings.*" This surprising phrase not only points to Jesus' authority to forgive sins, but is a foreshadowing of stories to come in which Jesus grants the authority to bind and loose both to Peter and the church (Mt. 16:19; 18:18).

But the conversations in the healing scenes not only emphasize Jesus' authority, they also demonstrate his compassion. Jesus is responsive to requests for healing. He can be interrupted by human need. The first healing scene is representative of the willingness of Jesus to serve others. "'Lord, if you choose, you can make me clean.' Jesus stretched out his hand and touched (the leper). 'I do choose. Be made clean!'" (8:3-4. cf. 8:7; 8:32; 9:2-3; 9:22; 9:27-28). In case we miss it, Matthew makes this point clear in the summary of the section, "When he saw the crowds, he had compassion for them, because they were harassed and helpless, like sheep without a shepherd." Jesus is the compassionate one spoken of by the prophet Isaiah, "He took our infirmities and bore our diseases" (8:17).

✻ Reflection and Application

1. What does it mean to call Jesus, "Lord"? What does the faith of the centurion teach you about "lordship"?

2. Matthew hoped that a harassed church would be encouraged by remembering Jesus as a responsive healer. Do we expect Jesus' compassionate ministry to continue in our churches? Do we have a sense of the risen Christ continuing his works of healing and compassion among his people?

I DESIRE MERCY, NOT SACRIFICE

Related to the emerging portrait of Jesus, we learn a lot about faith and discipleship in this section. The healing stories draw our eye not only to the authority of Jesus, but also to the faith of those healed. Several times the faith of the person being healed is highlighted (8:2; 8:11; 9:2; 9:22; 9:29). Jesus responds to faith. What kind of people follow Jesus? Those who by faith trust in his power.

Pictures of faith in the healing stories are supplemented by the two stories on discipleship (8:18-22; 9:9-17). In the first story, Matthew shortens material shared by Luke to emphasize the all-or-nothing nature of following Jesus (cf. Luke 9:57-62). Follow me! Let the dead bury the dead. Single minded faith is a trait of the true disciple.

The second discipleship account is lengthened (cf. Mark 2:13-17), giving it a certain prominence. Jesus calls a tax collector to follow him, bringing the charge that "he eats with tax collectors and sinners." Matthew follows Mark's account of this story, nearly verbatim, except at one strategic point. In verse 13 Matthew inserts Jesus' instructions to the Pharisees, "Go and learn what this means, 'I desire mercy, not sacrifice.'" This line, an allusion to sayings from Hosea and Micah, characterizes the difference between Jesus and the Pharisees. The program of the Pharisees, flying under the banner of "sacrifice," stands in contrast to Jesus who leads with "mercy."

What kind of people follow Jesus? Those who by faith trust in his power.

How do mercy and sacrifice stand in contrast with one another? We will see the differences as the story continues to unfold. For Micah and Hosea it reflected a misplaced confidence in religious observance as opposed to a lifestyle committed to the mercy of God. When sacrifice triumphs over mercy, religion becomes more important than God and neighbor. Andre Resner refers to this line, unique to Matthew, as the first great commission in Matthew's gospel.[1] What a striking observation! Disciples of Jesus heed the first great commission, "Go and learn mercy."

---

[1] Andre Resner, "I Desire Mercy, Not Sacrifice," Presentation at Northwest Expositor's Seminar, Beaverton, Oregon, 1997.

🌿 Reflection and Application

1. What problems might the church encounter if it practices the second "great commission" without obeying the first?

2. Non-Christians have plenty of experience with those attempting to do the second great commission apart from the first. What is their critique of "religious people"? Might they be telling us what it means to value sacrifice over mercy?

NEW WINE, OLD WINESKINS

Matthew connects the story of the calling of Matthew with the sayings about fasting and wineskins. Jesus' disciples do not fast because his ministry is unique in the history of God's redeeming work. His work is new wine which inevitably bursts old wineskins. Here we see the theme of new and old. Jesus' new ministry cannot be contained by the old standards practiced by the scribes and the Pharisees. In with the new, out with the old? Not quite. Matthew's use of this story also demonstrates Jesus' concern for the old wineskin. In comparison to Mark's account which seems to focus more on the loss of the spilled wine (2:22), Matthew seems just as concerned with the fate of the old wineskin: "the skins burst, and the wine is spilled, *and the skins are destroyed.*" The old and new are both affirmed in Matthew's account. Matthew's account ends with a phrase unique to his gospel, "but new wine is put into fresh wineskins, and *so both are preserved*" (8:17). Jesus did not come to abolish the law, but to fulfill it. Ironically, the new wineskins of Jesus serve to preserve the old.

This theme of old and new is also present in the first two healing stories in this section (8:1-13). In the first, Jesus tells the healed leper to "go show yourself to the priest, and offer the gift that Moses commanded, for a proof to the people" (8:4). Here, Jesus upholds the law and honors the old. The next story, however, features the faith of a Gentile. Jesus marvels at the centurion's faith, "Truly I say to you, not even in Israel have I found such faith" (8:10). Jesus models for Matthew's church both adherence to the law (old), and an openness to the faith of Gentiles (new). In the emerging kingdom of heaven, Gentiles will come from east and west to enjoy table fellowship (a major issue for Jews of Jesus' day) with Abraham, while those born sons of the kingdom will be thrown into outer darkness (8:10-12).

🌿 Reflection and Application

1. Matthew's church is one in the throes of transition. How important is it to affirm both old and new during transition? What does the new provide? What does the old provide?

2. Sometimes it is difficult for a church to preserve tradition *and* be concerned with outsiders. Jesus does both in the first two healing stories. Which is your church more focused on? What advice might Jesus have for your church in recovering a focus on both?

A CLOSER LOOK

1. "Go and learn what this means, 'I desire mercy not sacrifice.'" This "great commission" is vital to what it means to be a disciple in the gospel of Matthew. Decide this week to live by the rule of mercy. How many of your relationships are dictated by a spirit of sacrifice over mercy? This is not a direction learned overnight. It takes constant diligence with regard to motives and often calls us away from self-interest.

2. In a culture of self-reliance, it is sometimes difficult to look to another for our wholeness and sense of well-being. The question Jesus asks the blind men might be a good one for us as well: "Do you believe I can do this?" Do we believe that Jesus can bring healing to our lives? Will we trust him with the pain and illness we encounter? We have been called to a demanding discipleship under the lordship of Jesus. Allow him to be not only lord, but also healer.

5

LIKE SHEEP IN THE MIDST OF WOLVES

MATTHEW 10:1-42

HUNGER AND THIRST

A wagon train makes very little progress toward its destination when the wagons are circled to ward off hostile attack. Reading this section of Matthew leaves the impression that the original readers know all too well what it is to have the wagons circled. In this unit we will hear Jesus tell the twelve, "I send you out like sheep in the midst of wolves" (10:16). You don't have to be a sheep to appreciate this metaphor of danger!

While there are always risks in crying "wolf," many of us are aware of a changing environment for ministry in our culture. While it once appeared that our culture supported and even promoted Christian values, we now minister in a context that is indifferent and sometimes even hostile to those values. One response to an increasingly hostile ministry environment is to seek refuge by withdrawing into a cloistered life and minimizing contact with anyone not displaying a fish on their car or yellow pages ad. While safety and distinctiveness might be maintained by such a strategy, drawbacks exist. It is difficult to be mission-minded when you are in a defensive posture, especially if you must think of your "attackers" as your mission field. It is hard to think of your "enemies" simultaneously as "prospects." Where does a beleaguered church find the courage to be mission minded? Jesus' words speak across time both to Matthew's church and ours in addressing this issue.

HEARING THE STORY

This section represents Matthew's second teaching discourse (see unit two). Many of the sayings in this section are unique to Matthew, not appearing in Mark, Luke, or John. Unique sayings and stories often provide great insight into the purpose of the author. For instance, Luke's pronounced emphasis on wealth and poverty finds clearest expression in parables like the rich fool (12:13-21) and the rich man and Lazarus (16:19-31), stories both unique to Luke. As you read, pay particular attention to verses 5-6, 17-25, 40-42. These verses are found only in Matthew and may provide valuable insight into the gospel's audience and purpose.

✢ Reflection and Application

1. How do the verses unique to Matthew contribute to our overall understanding of

the gospel? Do they build on themes already established? What might they be telling us about the circumstances of the original readers of this gospel?

2. What themes or refrains seem prominent in this section? What is the function of this speech? Does it warn? Does it reassure? Does it challenge? All of the above?

THEY WILL FLOG YOU IN THEIR SYNAGOGUES

Military recruiting posters tend to say things like, "See the world!" and "Be all you can be." Recruits might be less eager if ads read "let us paint a target on your chest." In choosing inviting images from Matthew, we would certainly choose "Come to me all you who are weary and over burdened and I will give you rest" over "I send you out like sheep in the midst of wolves." The latter is not a very reassuring image. Unless perhaps you already see yourself as a sheep surrounded by wolves. The idea that your current trouble was previously foreseen and is somehow part of a larger cause might prove reassuring.

The mission of the twelve is to the "lost sheep of the house of Israel" (10:6). This description of Israel points back to the summary in 9:36. Jesus has "compassion on them, because they were harassed and helpless, like sheep without a shepherd." In this text, Jesus also calls for laborers to send out into a plentiful harvest (9:37-38). What is the field that is ripe? Is it Israel? Is it the nations? Or both? It is clear that a mission to the Gentiles is not a part of the commission of the twelve. But how would Matthew's church read this text? Matthew's gospel ends with a call to go to all nations making disciples. Is the mission to the lost sheep of the house of Israel a secondary concern after the resurrection of Jesus? My sense is that Mathew's church read this text as an ongoing mission. Jesus' prediction that his followers would be handed over to "sanhedrins" to be flogged in synagogues, and dragged before governors and kings seem to have both Jewish and Gentile audiences in mind. Few doubt that Matthew's church faced the very real consequences of being cut off from the synagogue and knew the pain of brother betraying brother, father turning against child, and child against father (10:21).

We should not lightly pass over the language of family conflict in this text. In our world, we are aquainted with families, even marriages, that include members of different faiths. Religion, we think, is an individual or private matter. But in Jesus' world identity was bound up in family and clan. Security and viability were guaranteed by the ties of kinship. The decision to follow Jesus apart from these ties would brand one a deviant and an outcast and would incur serious consequences. Jesus realizes the social implications of the decision to follow him. "I have not come to bring peace, but a sword. For I have come to set a man against his father, and a daughter against her mother. . . and one's foes will be members of one's own household" (10:34-36). Matthew's church is facing the harsh realities of the decision to follow Jesus—realities he foresaw and invited. Not only are they to survive in this environment, but they are to think of the lost sheep of Israel as a mission field. Jesus addresses both the twelve

32

and Matthew's church when he says "I am sending you out like sheep in the midst of wolves."

✢ Reflection and Application

1. Most of us made the decision to follow Jesus without any loss of social standing or viability. Is that an advantage or disadvantage?

2. Do you know people who have lost the support of family because of their decision to follow Jesus? How would you characterize their faith? What allows them to continue without the support of kinship?

SO HAVE NO FEAR OF THEM

Jesus envisions a new community, a new kind of kinship, that is based not on blood ties but upon a shared confession. "Whoever acknowledges me before others, I will also acknowledge before my Father in heaven" (10:32). The language of allegiance to Jesus is striking and demanding. Whoever denies Jesus before others will be denied before the Father in heaven. Whoever loves family more than Jesus is not worthy of him. Whoever finds their life will lose it. Whoever releases their life for Jesus' sake will find it. Through new allegiances, the followers of Jesus find themselves belonging to a more substantial family – the family of the Father in heaven.

Jesus' followers are now sent into a dangerous world with more than just warnings. They are a new family with a heavenly identity. Though they are being sent out like sheep in the midst of wolves, the followers of Jesus are not to fear. Fear in a dangerous mission setting is diminished when the mission is seen from God's perspective. Three beliefs cast out fear in this text. First, the Spirit of God will provide the words when Jesus' followers are dragged before councils and kings. Second, God sees in secret and uncovers everything that is hidden. Third, there is something worse than bodily death – the death of a soul, and the destiny of a soul is God's business. Have confidence in God. Do not be afraid of the wolves.

Finally, Jesus' followers know that they have fellowship with him as they minister in difficult circumstances. A follower is not above the teacher. If they accuse Jesus of being Beelzebul, why should his followers expect different treatment? It is enough for the disciple to be like the teacher (10:24-25). Disciples are not sent anywhere the teacher is unwilling to go. Here we find the implicit promise of Emmanuel – God with us. Mission in Jesus' name is no safe enterprise, but the call can be answered with the sure knowledge that "the one who endures to the end will be saved" (10:22).

✢ Reflection and Application

1. We hear a lot these days about family values. In light of these verses, what would

Jesus make of our talk of family values? Is it possible to make family too important?

2. What is the relationship between trust and fear? Which is easier for us, trust or fear? What belief about God expressed in this text would allow you to be more free of fear?

WHOEVER WELCOMES YOU WELCOMES ME

Okay, send me on a dangerous mission, but let me take a few of the comforts of home! The sparse packing list for the twelve in verses 9-10 strikes us as poor planning. In Jesus' day, however, such meager provision was expected of itinerant prophets and philosophers. Jesus' stated concern that the disciples received freely and, therefore, should give freely is often held up as an ideal for travelling preachers (10:8). Notice that Paul follows this impulse, offering the gospel to his hearers "free of charge" (1 Cor. 9:14). While Paul conforms to this social convention, he treads across another by working with his own hands and refusing payment for his preaching. Paul's offering of the gospel free of charge and working with his own hands sounds like a consistent stance to our modern ears. However, the social value of reciprocity so crucial to order in the ancient world demanded payment of some sort, usually hospitality and enough provision for the next leg of the journey. Paul's refusal of the patronage of the Corinthians might have been a challenge to their sense of honor. Those sent to preach in the ancient world did not do it for worldly advantage, but could expect their hearers to provide for their immediate needs.

Jesus seems very concerned with issues of hospitality and rejection as he sends the twelve. For a community to refuse welcome to an itinerant preacher was a serious affront. In such cities the twelve are told to "shake the dust off your feet," a recipro-cal act of rejection. The disciples are not to take matters into their own hands and seek some kind of retribution, but instead are to trust in God to deal with them in the great judgement. On the other hand, "whoever welcomes you, welcomes me," Jesus proclaims, "and whoever welcomes me, welcomes the one who sent me" (10:40-42). Those extending hospitality will receive nothing less than the rewards of the righteous and the prophets.

Jesus sends the twelve with the good news of the kingdom. Their ministry of healing, raising the dead, cleansing lepers, and casting out demons placed them in continuity with the ministry of Jesus. The threat of councils and kings, and rejection by family and cities cannot negate the reality that in Jesus "the kingdom of heaven has come near" (10:7-8). Matthew's church is encouraged to do more than just survive. It is to think of itself as an extension of the mission of Jesus, proclaiming and enacting the realities of the nearness of the kingdom of heaven.

1. Does your church spend more time talking about separating from the world or meaningfully engaging the world? What are the greatest obstacles you face as a church in being mission focused in your own community? What would Jesus say to us as he sends us into our neighborhoods?

2. Do we have anything to learn from the culture of Jesus' day about taking no gold, silver, or copper in our belts as we go into the world?

A Closer Look

1. Not all of us are sent to the "lost sheep of the house of Israel." However, all of us are called on to acknowledge Jesus before others. While we might not explicitly deny Jesus, my hunch is that we miss many opportunities to acknowledge him before others. Think of at least one area where you could acknowledge Jesus in a more explicit way. Pray for the courage to confess his name.

2. Matthew's gospel constantly calls our allegiances into question. Though it is a difficult saying of Jesus, spend the week praying over the phrase, "whoever loves father or mother more than me is not worthy of me." Do your best not to spiritualize this phrase. Let it have its provocative force. Share with a brother or sister your impressions from a week with this phrase.

6
I WILL GIVE YOU REST

MATTHEW 11:2-12:50

HUNGER AND THIRST

R est. Is there a more attractive word in our day and age? We live hurried and harried lives. We are tantalized by so many things that offer more enjoyment or more productivity– we feel we can hardly say no. Our inability to refuse opportunity stretches life to the breaking point. To relieve this stress we seek diversions in entertainment, travel, and ever more elaborate vacations. While these diversions might provide respite and some release away from our frenetic lives, they often do not provide rest. Rest needs to be more than a vacation. It is more than a nap. True rest gives us peace. In an age that offers more anxiety than peace, rest for the soul is a welcome invitation.

In an age that offers more anxiety than peace, rest for the soul is a welcome invitation.

HEARING THE TEXT

A good story teller uses repetition to leave clues as to the meaning of a story. Sometimes repetition serves as foreshadowing, reminding the reader over and over of details that will be important to understand the end of the story. Other times repetition allows the story to make a point without a comment or aside by the narrator. This section is rich with recurring ideas and phrases. Some we have already noticed, others appear here for the first time. As you read this section aloud, make mental notes of the significant words, phrases, or themes that we have already seen.

🌿 Reflection and Application

1. What repeating themes did you find? What do you think Matthew is trying to communicate in these instances of repetition?

2. Notice again the verses in this section that are unique to Matthew's gospel: 11:14; 11:20, 23b-24; 11:28-30; 12:5-7; 12:11-12; 12:16-21; 12:22-23; 12:27-28, 30, 33-34,36. What do you make of these unique elements? Do they provide clues to Matthew's purpose? How would these unique sections sound to Matthew's audience?

THE KINGDOM HAS SUFFERED VIOLENCE

A task of leadership in times of transition is to clarify allegiances. In the last chapter we heard Jesus warn his disciples that they were being sent out like sheep in the midst of wolves, and that some of the wolves might be family members. Following Jesus means acceptance by some and rejection by others. Not only is this true for Jesus, but for all of God's prophets (5:11-12; 23:29-36). The report of John the Baptist's arrest and imprisonment at the hands of Herod reinforces this point (11:2-19). Though imprisoned, Jesus claims that "among those born of women no one has arisen greater than John the Baptist" (11:11). Matthew's community should not read John's persecution, or theirs, as a sign of God's disfavor, or as evidence that they have misplaced allegiances. To the contrary, their rejection is nothing less than solidarity with God's line of prophets culminating in John and Jesus.

Jesus is gathering a people of new allegiances. The choice for Matthew's church is clear. Jesus challenges them, "Whoever is not with me is against me, and whoever does not gather with me scatters" (12:30). "Who is my mother and who are my brothers?" Jesus asks those who have been rejected by family members. "Here are my mother and my brothers! For whoever does the will of my Father in heaven is my brother and sister and mother" (12:48-50). This is a new kinship based on discipleship. These are not the wise, intelligent, or powerful of the world, but the "little ones," those humble enough to see God's revelation in Jesus (11:25-27). Moreover, the woes against Chorazin and Bethsaida suggest that those who have done violence against the kingdom will be rejected by God on the last day (11:20-24). Matthew's church should choose allegiances wisely (11:19).

⅔ Reflection and Application

1. Jesus offers a new family based not in blood ties, but in discipleship. Which is thicker, blood (kinship) or water (those joined by baptism into a new family)?

2. Have you received things you needed from the church that you didn't or couldn't receive from your family?

TAKE MY YOKE AND LEARN FROM ME

Jesus offers rest to a harried church. "Come unto me...and I will give you rest for your souls." The great invitation (11:28-30), verses unique to Matthew's gospel, pulls together several prominent themes. Jesus, as Israel's teacher, is calling them to a demanding righteousness. "Take my yoke upon you, and learn from me," he invites. He also speaks again as the compassionate shepherd, "I am gentle and humble in heart."

Notice that Jesus offers rest not by throwing off all yokes, but precisely through bearing his yoke. Wearing a yoke hardly suggests rest or freedom. A yoke is a burden and requires submission. It does not immediately bring to mind rest. Yet, that is precisely what Jesus offers. His yoke is easy and his burden light, not because it is unimpressive (a righteousness exceeding, a narrow path), but because Jesus is gentle and humble in heart. He is not like the scribes and Pharisees who "tie up heavy burdens, hard to bear, and lay them upon the shoulders of others: but they themselves are unwilling to lift a finger to move them" (23:4). While the yoke of the scribes and Pharisees wearies, Jesus' yoke actually brings rest for the soul because he helps bear burdens.

⁂ Reflection and Application

1. Our furiously paced society leaves us longing for rest. What strategies do we typically choose for providing rest? How is Jesus' offer of rest different?

2. We live in a society that thinks of all yokes as oppressive. Yet, the irony of our culture is that free of all yokes we seem more rest-less. Can a yoke really provide rest? Are there possible advantages to the soul in submitting to a yoke? How would you tell your neighbor that putting on the yoke of Jesus actually provides rest?

IF YOU HAD KNOWN, "MERCY, NOT SACRIFICE"

How can a righteousness that exceeds that of the scribes and Pharisees be a light burden? No story in Matthew's gospel demonstrates the difference between Jesus and the scribes and Pharisees more than the sabbath controversy in 12:1-14. Matthew has lifted the story from its sequence in the gospel of Mark (2:23-28) and placed it in a more prominent place, connecting it strategically to the great invitation. This story demonstrates Jesus' approach to the law and to the important task of binding and loosing. His yoke is easy because Jesus understands the place and priority of mercy over sacrifice.

Remember the first great commission we noticed in 9:13, "Go and learn... mercy, not sacrifice." As with that story, only Matthew records Jesus' words in 12:17, "If you had known what this means, 'I desire mercy and not sacrifice,' you would not have condemned the guiltless." The reappearance of this strategic phrase alerts us to the importance of this story in the unfolding of the gospel. It is a case study in binding and loosing, a practice crucial to the order and survival of Matthew's community.

The specific dispute in 12:1-8 centers around the disciples harvesting grain on the sabbath and whether or not this transgressed the prohibition of work on the sabbath found in Exodus 34:21. While Mark records the Pharisees' concern as a question (2:24), Matthew reports their words as an accusation (12:2), heightening the tension in the narrative and emphasizing their own interpretation of the law. Matthew moves beyond Mark's account by providing a reason for the disciples' activity – they were hungry.

Matthew's portrayal of Jesus in this story emphasizes his expertise in matters

38

pertaining to the law. According to Jesus, the disciples' action is no different than that of David and his men who "unlawfully" ate the bread of presence because they were hungry. Mark and Luke also cite this precedent in their account of this confrontation. However, only Matthew notes Jesus' use of the law to point out the provision for priests to do extra work on the sabbath (cf. Lev 24:8; Num 28:9-10). In comparison to Jesus, the Pharisees prove to be poor interpreters of the law. Their lack of comprehension comes from a faulty vantage point. They see Torah observance as an end in itself, whereas Jesus sees it as an expression of the character of God. The Pharisees are concerned with sacrifice, Jesus with mercy. Jesus does not nullify the yoke of sabbath observance, but through the eyes of mercy makes observance a light burden.

This merciful perspective is underscored in 12:9-14 when Jesus heals a man with a withered hand on the sabbath. Some rabbis taught that healing was allowable on the sabbath only in life-threatening situations. This healing clearly falls short of that stipulation. Jesus' own criteria is whether or not it is right to "do good" on the sabbath. Matthew again presents material unique to his gospel by citing the case of a sheep fallen in a ditch. The Essenes taught that in such a case the sheep was to be left in the ditch. Jesus agrees with the Pharisees understanding that it would be permissable to rescue the sheep and turns their interpretation against them. The logic is clear and "withering" (pun intended). If it is "good" to rescue a sheep, how much more to heal a person on the sabbath. The significance of this episode for understanding Matthew's gospel is underscored by Matthew's report of the Pharisees' reaction: "The Pharisees went out and conspired against him, how to destroy him" (12:14). The die is cast.

One final observation remains. The Pharisees attempt to bind the disciples to their interpretation of the law. Jesus, in contrast, looses them to harvest grain on the sabbath. Matthew's church recognizes in this story Jesus' authority to bind and loose in relation to the Torah. Something greater than the temple is here – Jesus, himself. They also see binding and loosing done faithfully around the standard of mercy. Jesus' care for the hunger of the disciples reveals him as gentle and humble in heart.

❧ Reflection and Application

1. While the language of binding and loosing might be strange to us, the concept is not. We discuss in our churches whether or not certain passages are binding on us today, or in every situation. Do we bind and loose more like Jesus or the Pharisees? What examples can you think of that support your understanding?

2. Here we see mercy and sacrifice contrasted in the practice of Jesus and the Pharisees. How has the way of sacrifice been further defined in this story?

39

1. We often think the way to rest is to relieve ourselves of all responsibility or by disengaging from life. Christian rest, rest for the soul, comes through engaging the yoke of Jesus. Recall again the images and challenges of the Sermon on the Mount. What will you do for "rest" this week?

2. Take an inventory of your allegiances. Transitions call for clear allegiances. We can't rest until we know whose we are. Answer again the invitation of Jesus. Come to him, and only him.

7

SCRIBES TRAINED FOR THE KINGDOM

MATTHEW 13:1-53

HUNGER AND THIRST

Albert Einstein is reported to have commented, "Imagination is better than knowledge." While that seems heretical to those of us trained by the modern world to value facts, I think the teaching of Jesus exhibits great imagination. Imagination allows new worlds to emerge, worlds that fall just beyond the horizon of our viewing.

Long before John Lennon sang "Imagine," Jesus imagined a new world where things become on earth as they are in heaven. To live in this world after the way of Jesus calls for faithful imagination, learning to see beyond the horizon of the powers of this world to a new reality embodied by Jesus. Often, we need gifted guides to help us see with kingdom eyes. Matthew's church knew well the influence of Jewish scribes who interpreted the law for them. Now in the transition away from the synagogue, they need Christian scribes who will show them the surprising world of the kingdom present in the ministry of Jesus.

HEARING THE TEXT

"Jesus told the crowds all these things in parables; without a parable he told them nothing" (13:34). Why are parables so central to his teaching ministry? The burden of Jesus' teaching is nothing less than the creation of an alternative kingdom. Parables are indispensable to kingdom creation in a fallen world.

The parables of Jesus take familiar scenes and stand them on their head. But for many of us, the parables are so familiar they have lost their sense of surprise. Listen again from a new perspective. Listen as a member of Matthew's church.

❧ Reflection and Application

1. How do the parables fit together in this chapter? Would you group them in any particular ways?

2. As you read this section from the perspectives of Matthew's church, what new insights did you gain?

BLESSED ARE YOUR EYES FOR THEY SEE

Is there anything more delicious than insider information? We love secret handshakes and code words, inside jokes and exclusive information. Bonds of identity are formed through shared information, especially information not made available to all. Matthew's church might be struggling, but they know the secrets of the kingdom of heaven. They have ears to hear. They are good soil.

Explanation for why Jesus teaches in parables is given twice in this section (13:10-17; 34-35). The second simply cites Psalm 78 as an anticipation of Jesus' teaching. Again, Jesus' ministry follows the familiar traces of Scripture. He fulfills Old Testament expectations. The first explanation, however, suggests that parables divide people into two categories – those for whom the kingdom is prepared, and those who will not receive it. The hidden nature of a parable keeps those hard of heart from seeing and hearing lest they turn and be healed. This is certainly a difficult saying of Jesus. Yet, the theme of hardening appears throughout Scripture as a means to God's ends (cf. Ex. 10:1, Is. 6:9-10, Rom. 11:25). God uses those who mistakenly think they see to serve his own purposes. For the disciples, and for Matthew's church, this helps to explain why not all seed produces kingdom growth – why not all those who look for the Messiah find him. The parables function to sort insiders from outsiders.

Matthew emphasizes this insider/outsider function by having Jesus explain the parables only to the disciples. While he tells the parable of the soils to the "great crowds" (13:1), he explains it to the gathered disciples (13:10). The same dynamic is repeated with the parable of the wheat and weeds as Jesus moves into a private residence. Here he explains the meaning exclusively to the disciples (13:36-43). They are the insiders, the little ones, to whom the kingdom has been revealed. Overhearing this conversation, Matthew's church becomes insiders as well. They know the "secrets of the kingdom of heaven," and so have special identity and belonging.

Sharing secrets forms and maintains identity, but it can also lead to exclusivism and arrogance. The tendency of insiders is to identify and "weed out" those not initiated into the secret. The parable of the wheat and weeds makes it clear that the task of the slaves of the householder is not to separate weeds and wheat. The violence of "weeding" will not only exclude others, but damage insiders as well. To choose another metaphor from this section, the business of sorting fish belongs to the angels of God at the end of the age and is not the work of the church (13:47-50). This parable also might explain to Matthew's persecuted church why God delays in punishing their persecutors.

❧ Reflection and Application

These parables seem to walk a tightrope between upholding the privileged status of insiders without becoming exclusive and judgmental. This is a difficult stance to maintain. How have our churches done in walking the tightrope? What aspect of the parables do we need to hear most in our churches today?

THE SMALL AND THE SIGNIFICANT

It quite possibly took an act of great imagination for Matthew's church to feel it was part of something significant. They went from belonging to a centuries old religion to forming a new upstart faith. Banned from synagogues, they found themselves a persecuted minority, cut off from historic ties important for protection. Probably smaller than the mother synagogues they were separating from, they could easily appear to be on the wrong side of history.

However, appearances may not be the best indicator of the presence of the kingdom of God. Take, for instance, the mustard seed, the smallest of all seeds, which eventually grows into an impressive shrub. Powerful kingdom realities might be present in small beginnings though hidden from plain view. The power of the kingdom may be hidden like yeast in flour. Though hidden and small, the yeast leavens the entire batch of dough.

Matthew's church does not yet know what it will become. They do know, however, how they will fare in the entire sweep of history. At the end of the age the good fish go in the baskets and the bad are thrown away. At the end of the age, the weeds and wheat are separated and the weeds burned. These pictures serve to encourage a small, struggling church that their commitments and allegiances to Jesus place them in a role of significance in the kingdom of heaven – a significance to be honored at the end of the age.

❧ Reflection and Application

1. How do we evaluate whether or not something is significant? What criteria do we typically bring to judge whether or not a church or movement is successful? Do we judge by appearances, believing that bigger is better? What criteria for success is held up by these parables?

2. Do you know any "mustard seed" stories? Have you seen God do big things through insignificant beginnings? How do stories like these build our faith?

TREASURE NEW AND OLD

Notice that Matthew places the parables of the treasure in the field and the pearl of great price between statements concerning eternal punishment and reward (13:36-43; 47-50). The parables of judgement arrest our attention. Who wouldn't choose a face that shines like sun in the kingdom of heaven over a furnace of fire and weeping and gnashing of teeth? When stated in these terms the pursuit of the kingdom, whatever the cost , makes great sense. Perhaps this is why Matthew has grouped these parables together.

The parables of the treasure in the field are notable for two images: the value of the possession that is sought, and the obsession of the purchaser. Both characterize life in the kingdom. The parable of the pearl of great price connects easily with the modern reader. We think the pearl merchant was wise to sell everything for such a rare find. The parable of the treasure in the field, however, contains meanings lost to a modern mindset. We live by the credo, "finders keepers, losers weepers." The rabbis, however, considered the type of behavior described in the parable as unethical. The man finding treasure in the field has no right to it. He should disclose the information before a purchase of the property is executed. Instead he buries the treasure again and with joy goes and sells all that he has to purchase the field. Jesus' hearers would have been shocked and surprised by the behavior of the one who found the treasure. But the parable is not used by Jesus as a morality tale. Rather, the treasure of the kingdom motivates single-minded behavior outside the norms of what is expected. So great is the treasure and the joy in discovery that those who happen upon the kingdom are completely willing to reorient their lives to the reality of the great find. Those whose faces will shine radiantly in the kingdom of heaven are the single-minded who seek first the kingdom, those whose eye is full of light and singleness of vision.

The theme of treasure is picked up in the final verses of this teaching section (13:51-53). As all good treasure hunters know, X marks the spot. We mentioned in unit 2 that Matthew arranged five teaching discourses throughout the gospel to form a *chi* (looks like our letter "X"). These parables on the kingdom, as the third discourse, occupy the middle of the *chiasm*, and, therefore, hold a strategic place in the gospel. Jesus' statement at the conclusion of these teachings is unique to Matthew. "Every scribe who has been trained for the kingdom of heaven is like the master of a household who brings out of his treasure what is new and what is old" (13:52). Jesus is such a scribe, one who interprets the ways of God for others. His teachings are simultaneously new and in keeping with the law and traditions of Israel's faith. Some see in this verse a description of the author of Matthew. His gospel holds together old and new, and therefore, faithfully represents the concerns of Jesus and the kingdom. This saying also serves as a description for the type of teacher Matthew's church community can trust in a time of transition.

Transition requires an acceptance of new realities. Successful transition, however, requires more than just an acceptance of new treasures. Successful transitions find treasure in the old as well. Wise kingdom scribes do not sever ties with the past in favor of embracing the new. Instead they find both new and old treasure mutually enriching. This is the way of the kingdom. The kingdom comes near to us in the midst of old realities and transforms them. The kingdom, however, also comes in ways beyond things we have seen and observed The mercies of God are new every morning. Any servant of the kingdom values things both old and new.

⅋ Reflection and Application

We have noted in several places Matthew's stress on identifying faithful leaders. In this strategic chapter in the heart of the gospel, the identity of a kingdom scribe takes center stage. How should leaders today think about the categories of old and new? In a time of transition, what are the dangers of placing too much stress on things old? What are the dangers of placing too much stress on things new? Have you seen leaders err on both sides of this equation?

A Closer Look

1. Parables ask us to adjust our vision to take into account new and surprising realities. Use this week to pray for new eyes to see more clearly the perspectives of the kingdom. Look for mustard seeds.

2. The parables of the treasure in the field and the pearl of great price remind us that the kingdom is found only through single-minded pursuit. Take an inventory of your energies. Is the kingdom your treasure? Choose again to seek first the kingdom. Share with a brother or sister the result of your self-inventory and the path of repentance you hope to follow.

8

ON THIS ROCK I WILL BUILD MY CHURCH

MATTHEW 13:54-17:27

HUNGER AND THIRST

One of my favorite movies is *Groundhog Day*. Bill Murray plays a man who is stuck reliving the same day over and over again. Early in the movie he discovers that this can work to his advantage. He lives each day satisfying his own selfish desires and manipulating people to serve that end. My favorite scene portrays Murray in a diner stuffing his face with food and cigarettes, a portrait of self-indulgence. The female object of Murray's affections, played by Andie McDowell, finds this loathsome. Murray, his mouth filled with cake, asks "you think I'm egocentric?" McDowell replies, "its your defining characteristic." Murray's attempts at self-satisfaction end in emptiness. He's trapped in the day with only himself and his desires. The movie turns on several scenes in which Murray tries to kill himself to exit this endless day.

The Bible suggests that such egocentrism, self-centeredness, is everyone's defining characteristic. How can God save people from themselves? Salvation, it seems, can only come by being called to lay our lives aside for the sake of others. We need others to be saved. We need a church.

HEARING THE STORY

I have chosen two stories from this section which are found also in Mark and Luke that feature Peter: Jesus' walking on water and Peter's confession of Jesus (14:22-33; 16:13-23). I choose them not simply because they highlight Peter, but because Matthew provides information the other gospel accounts do not. By looking at Peter in these stories we will gain even greater insight into the purpose of Matthew's gospel. Read the entire section if time allows to get a sense for how these stories fit into the overall flow of the gospel.

✎ Reflection and Application

1. The only miracle story included in all four gospels is the feeding of the 5,000. Notice that in Matthew it follows the story of Herod's banquet, which results in the beheading of John the Baptist. What contrasts would you make between the banquet Herod provides and the one Jesus hosts?

2. Compare Matthew 15:21-28 with Mark 7:24-30. What differences exist between the two accounts? What would explain the things Matthew emphasizes and the things he chooses not to report? How might this story encourage both Jewish and Gentile members of Matthew's community?

THOSE IN THE BOAT WORSHIPPED HIM

The sea, or the deep, occupies a prominent but notorious place in the pages of Scripture. In the ancient world the sea was the place of chaos, an enemy to life. Even moderns know the primordial fear of drowning in uncontrollable waters. A prominent image of God in Scripture is the one who controls the sea. God brings order to the powers of chaos in creation. In the Psalms God is the one who raises and calms the sea. In the writings of the Essenes, the images of drowning and rescue were used to refer to times of persecution. God rescues those tossed about in the sea of persecution.

The stories in which Jesus shows mastery over the sea demonstrate his identity as Son of God. The details of this story bear this out in plain fashion. When the disciples see Jesus walking on the water, they cried out for fear, "It is a ghost!" (14:26). Jesus' answer, "It is I," appears in the Old Testament in several places as a divine name (Exod 3:14; Deut 32:39; Isa 41:4; 43:10). Isaiah 43 seems to especially stand in the background of this text. There the LORD exhorts his people, "Do not fear...When you pass through the waters I will be with you . . . I, I am the LORD, and besides me there is no Savior" (1-2, 11). In this story, Jesus acts like God for the salvation of his people. While Mark's account leaves the disciples a bewildered lot not recognizing Jesus' identity, Matthew portrays the disciples responding properly to him. They worship him and confess, "Truly you are the Son of God" (14:32).

Only in Matthew does Peter ask to join Jesus on the water. We admire Peter's courage, his willingness to step out of the boat to be with Jesus and experience his power. However, we also recognize all too well his doubting faith that causes him to sink. Peter's cry is ours as well, "Lord, save me!" (14:30). While we might be tempted to place the focus of this story on Jesus' rebuke of Peter, "You of little faith, why did you doubt?" the proper emphasis belongs on the saving work of Jesus. In Joseph's dream the angel declared that Jesus would save his people. Here his saving power is demonstrated, even in the midst of a stormy sea. The Son of God has power to save!

⁂ Reflection and Application

1. "When you pass through the waters I will be with you." The phrase from Isaiah 43 fits so well Matthew's message exemplified in this story. How does this story continue the theme of Emmanuel – "God with us"?

2. Peter's failure in the storm seems to be related to his recognition of how strong the wind was blowing. What should our focus be during times of storm? Why

do we become distracted by the wind? Is there grace in this story for people overly impressed with the size of the waves?

JESUS BEGAN TO SHOW HIS DISCIPLES THAT HE MUST SUFFER

Peter's confession that Jesus is the Messiah, the Son of the living God forms one of the dramatic high points in the gospel (16:13-28). Jesus' identity is fully and faithfully proclaimed. Peter's confession does not originate with human observation. This confession recognizes heavenly perspectives, and for that Peter is blessed (16:16). However, Jesus is not anxious for just anyone to define what it means for him to be God's Messiah. He sternly orders the disciples not to tell anyone, lest his identity and mission be misconstrued. Indeed, Peter justifies Jesus' fear just a few verses after his marvelous confession. While Peter states the words correctly, he fails to understand what it means for Jesus to be the Messiah. For Jesus, his identity as Messiah is bound up in his suffering, death, and resurrection. Peter sees this as a failure, takes Jesus aside and rebukes him! "Why all this negative thinking? Why would God allow the story to end in failure? Have a little faith, here." Jesus returns the rebuke. "Get behind me, Satan! You are a stumbling block to me" (16:23). Though Peter's confession is from heaven, his understanding of Jesus' mission is all flesh and blood.

> *Jesus' death is not an unfortunate twist of fate. It is the very plan of God through which Jesus will save.*

This story is the first of three in which Jesus predicts his death, corrects the disciples' misunderstandings, and then teaches on the nature of discipleship (16:13-28; 17:22-18:4; 20:17-27). Jesus' death is not an unfortunate twist of fate. It is the very plan of God through which Jesus will save. More than that, the sacrificial nature of his death is a model for discipleship. While the disciples are jockeying for places of prominence in a triumphant kingdom, Jesus is offering his life in sacrificial service. A disciple is not greater than the teacher. Just as Jesus is willing to bear the cross, his followers must be willing to take up their crosses and follow him. Jesus' death on the cross is not simply payment for sin. It reveals the very nature and character of God. Those who would be like God must learn, as the hymn suggests, "the power of a full self-sacrifice" ("When My Love to Christ Goes Weak")[1].

❧ Reflection and Application

1. What do we fear the most when we hear the words, "deny yourself, take up your cross, and follow me"? Do we fear losing our identity? Are we afraid that others

---

[1] John R. Wreford, "When My Love to Christ Grows Weak," 1837.

48

will constantly take advantage of us? Are we afraid that there is precious little power in a "full self-sacrifice"?

2. What dangers does the church face if it confesses properly Jesus' titles but misses the nature of his character? Is it possible to say all the right things about Jesus and still not represent him faithfully to the world? The titles "Messiah," and "Son of God" carry a lot of power. Can the church sometimes misrepresent the nature of kingdom power by focusing more on Jesus' titles than his mission?

ON THIS ROCK I WILL BUILD MY CHURCH

"You are Peter (*petros*), and on this rock (*petra*) I will build my church" (16:18). Them's fightin' words! This line from Matthew's gospel is one of the most disputed in all of Scripture. At the heart of much of the debate is Peter's role in the early church. Is Jesus giving Peter a place of prominent leadership above the others? Some argue for Peter's prominence, some against. Unfortunately, the dispute has generated more heat than light and this text is likely to remain controversial. Another, more recent debate centers around Jesus' use of the word church (*ecclesia*). Only in Matthew does Jesus speak of the church (*ecclesia*), a word not likely to have been a part of his primary vocabulary. Did Jesus envision a church distinct from the Jewish synagogue communities? Did Jesus envision a community at all?

This study guide will not solve the first issue in any definitive way. However, I would like to make one suggestion. The story of Peter's confession follows immediately upon Jesus' warning to the twelve concerning the teaching of the Pharisees and Sadducees (16:5-12). Warnings against the teachings of the Pharisees appear in other strategic points in Matthew's gospel. In 23:1-36 Jesus warns against those who sit on Moses' seat – a position of teaching authority. These hypocrites bind heavy burdens on others without lifting a finger to help loose them. They lock people out of the kingdom of heaven and refuse to enter themselves. They tithe their spices, but neglect the weightier matters of the law, including mercy. Elsewhere, Jesus accuses them of being more concerned with their traditions than with the word of God (15:1-20).

In this story, Peter stands in contrast to the scribes and Pharisees. Unlike them, he confesses teaching received directly from heaven, not the traditions of men. Unlike the scribes and Pharisees who lock people out, Peter is given the keys to extend to others the invitation of Jesus to receive freely the kingdom of heaven. He can faithfully bind and loose because he recognizes Jesus' true identity. Jesus' identification of Peter as the rock upon which he will build the church reminds us of the saying at the end of the Sermon on the Mount concerning the one who builds his house on the rock. The wise man hears Jesus' words and acts on them. With his confession, Peter represents that rock.

Given Jesus' warning later in the gospel concerning places of privilege and status (23:8-10), it is unlikely that he is exalting Peter to such a place here. Moreover, the process for binding and loosing spelled out in chapter 18 does not describe any role for congregational leaders. That authority rests with the church, not a figure like Peter. Therefore, it is likely that Peter represents here a Christian scribe, or teacher, who stands in contrast to the teachers of the synagogues.

This brings us to our second issue. It is inconceivable that Jesus could preach about the kingdom without anticipating some sort of alternative community. Jesus called twelve disciples precisely for the purpose of symbolizing the gathering of a renewed Israel. The profoundly challenging ethics of the Sermon on the Mount only make sense within the context of a community. Finally, Matthew's portrayal of the church is in keeping with the understanding of salvation in the rest of Scripture. God's desire to bless the nations always comes through the presence of a holy people who model his ways before the nations. In fact, if our defining problem before God is self-centeredness, then the only way we can be saved is to be called into the lives of others.

❧ Reflection and Application

Unlike the scribes and Pharisees who lock people out of the kingdom, Peter has been given the keys to the kingdom to allow people to enter. Can churches be guilty of acting more like the scribes and Pharisees than Peter? Can they become this way without knowing? What characteristics do churches have who "lock people out?"

A Closer Look

In the story of Peter's confession we gain valuable insight into the nature of discipleship. Who can follow Jesus? Those who are willing to lay down their own lives for Jesus and the sake of the kingdom. Do you trust your identity to Jesus? Are you willing to lose your life so that you might find it? Ask God to search your motives. Finally, God has called together a community to interrupt your sense of self-importance. Don't ignore the calling of God that comes in the need of your brother or sister.

9

WHERE TWO OR THREE ARE GATHERED

MATTHEW 18:1-19:2

HUNGER AND THIRST

Anne Lamott writes that refusing to forgive is a "little like eating rat poison and then waiting for the rat to die."[1] We know the power of being forgiven. True forgiveness is liberating. We also know the difficulty of forgiving. It is one thing to say to someone, "I forgive you." It is another thing to truly forgive them. Refusal to forgive robs everyone – offender and offended – of the possibility of new life. Knowing that, we still find it hard to show mercy. We'd rather eat the rat poison. Forgiveness may be the most complex and difficult human interaction. It may also be the one that teaches us most clearly what it means to be like God. In Matthew, Jesus has called his followers to a demanding righteousness. We cannot remain in this way without the practice of mercy, both God's and the church's.

HEARING THE TEXT

This text represents the fourth of Matthew's five teaching discourses. As with the other discourses, it features material unique to Matthew that reveals the intent of the evangelist. The observant reader recognizes 18:15-20 and 18:23-35 as exclusive material to Matthew and asks how it adds to the overall portrait being painted for Matthew's church. I will comment on these texts below. However, another interesting feature of this section is Matthew's use of materials common to other gospels. Notice, for instance, 18:12-13, an abbreviated version of the story of the lost sheep found also in Luke. Luke combines this parable with the stories of the lost coin and the prodigal son to paint a powerful picture of God's concern for the lost. Here the story highlights Jesus' concern for "little ones." The image of the shepherd searching for one lost sheep mirrors God's concern for "little ones." The gospel writers use the stories in different ways. Be sure to notice the stories that appear only in one of the gospels as well as the ones that are included by more than one of the authors. The unique uses of these stories give clues to the author's intention.

✺ Reflection and Application

1. Can all the teachings in this chapter fall under a single heading? What do they have in common?

---

[1] Anne Lamott, *Travelling Mercies: Some Thoughts on Faith*, (New York: Pantheon Books, 1999), 134.

2. Some of the verses in this section are very familiar to our ears. In fact, we often hear them apart from their larger context. As you read this section and heard familiar phrases in their original contexts, did anything surprise you? What stood out to you most in this chapter?

THERE I AM IN THE MIDST OF THEM

Matthew begins the gospel with the birth announcement of a child who will be called Emmanuel, or "God *with us.*" It ends with Jesus' dramatic promise to be "*with you* until the end of the age." In Jesus, God is with his people always. This is clearly an important theme in Matthew that we find worked out in a number of stories. Yet, the only other text that explicitly guarantees the presence of Jesus with his people is found here in 18:20. We cite this text often (mostly on Sunday evenings) as a general promise that Jesus is present to even two or three gathered in his name. However, the specific context of Matthew portrays Jesus present to his disciples in the context of binding and loosing. Jesus authorizes the church saying, "Whatever you bind on earth will be bound in heaven, and whatever you loose on earth will be loosed in heaven" (18:18). This is kingdom work of the first order. Jesus confers upon his followers the awesome ability to make it in heaven as it is on earth. Instead of looking to the scribes and Pharisees or to the synagogue community, Jesus urges his followers to take matters to the church. They are to proceed confidently in the knowledge that the risen one is authoritatively present in their midst.

This text immediately brings to mind Jesus' similar statement to Peter only two chapters earlier (16:19). What are we to make of Peter's authority to bind and loose in light of this text? It is interesting that the discipline process outlined here nowhere appeals to congregational leadership. The process moves from member, to two or three members, to the entire congregation. The church's ability to bind and loose does not depend on Peter or someone representing Peter. Though attention is given in Matthew to the development of kingdom scribes, the authority of the risen Christ does not reside primarily in a leader or in leaders, but in the community of faith. This will become even more evident in the final discourse.

✢ Reflection and Application

1. Does your church cite Matthew 18 as a model for dealing with sin or disrupted relationships? Does your church follow the model faithfully? Where do you think the model breaks down most often? Were you surprised to read that there is no specific role for church leaders in the process? Is this how things work in your congregation?

2. From the process described in verses 15-20, what do you think it means to bind someone? How might binding be related to Jesus' concern for a righteousness that exceeds that of the scribes and Pharisees? From this context, what do you

think loosing involves? How might this be related to Jesus' prayer, "forgive us our debts, because we forgive our debtors"?

SEVENTY-SEVEN TIMES

Never missing an opportunity, Peter follows Jesus' instructions regarding binding and loosing with a question concerning the limits of mercy. Peter offers to forgive his brother seven times. Seven here represents a complete number, a perfect number of times, an impressive commitment to mercy. Jesus pushes the commitment even further using the number seventy-seven. If seven represents complete forgiveness, seventy-seven represents unlimited mercy.

Mercy is the standard by which the king evaluates this servant.

The exchange between Jesus and Peter concerning forgiveness is followed by the parable of the unmerciful servant, a parable unique to Matthew. This story brings together many of the themes we have already seen running through the gospel. Mercy is the standard by which the king evaluates this servant. An unforgiving spirit brings the harshest characterization from the king, "You wicked servant!" He has not heeded the first great commission, "Go and learn what this means, 'I desire mercy, not sacrifice.'" The servant also reveals himself to be a hypocrite. Being forgiven, he refuses to forgive. His life stands outside the concern of the Lord's prayer, "Forgive us our debts, *because* we have forgiven our debtors." The parable serves as a giant exclamation point marking mercy as the first of all kingdom virtues.

The fact that the discussion between Jesus and Peter on forgiveness and this parable on mercy have been connected to the process for binding and loosing should not be underestimated. In fact, we typically characterize 18:15-20 as a process for "disfellowshipping" a church member. We often lose sight of the concern Jesus has for mercy, both in process and outcome. The goal of binding and loosing is to "gain your brother or sister." This demands the extension of mercy, even seventy-seven times. Moreover, the process, which begins privately, seems interested in protecting the dignity of the offending party, a merciful concern. Binding and loosing with the authority of heaven is serious business and could be used by some as an instrument of destruction rather than of mercy. Peter's question concerning forgiveness combined with the parable of the unmerciful servant guard our understanding of this important practice for the church.

✣ Reflection and Application

=======================================

1. Have we read Matthew 18:15-20 more as a process of discipline or mercy? Why? What would we recover if we thought of this more as a mercy process?

2. Do we really believe in unlimited forgiveness? I am often struck by statements of parents or relatives of victims in the sentencing phase of a murder trial. Often I hear, "I can never forgive…." I understand that feeling. I have also been amazed by Christians who have extended forgiveness to murderers in similar circumstances. What does God really expect from us?

WHOEVER HUMBLES HIMSELF

Few pictures of Jesus are more familiar to us than his receiving little children. "Little ones" are prominent in Matthew's gospel. Sometimes, as in this text, the designation "little ones" refers specifically to children. We have seen, however, that little ones can also refer to Jesus' followers, even the disciples. Why is this designation so important?

Little ones stand in need. In the case of children, we recognize that they are less able than adults to fend for themselves or protect themselves in a dangerous world. To live faithfully toward a little one is to live mercifully. To take advantage of a defenseless one is to live the opposite of mercy. Jesus' stern warnings concerning the abuse of little ones marks the boudaries of mercy for his followers. Those who treat little ones well possess the merciful character necessary to be great in the kingdom of heaven. This kingdom character is formed in people who see themselves as "little ones," or as ones who stand in need of God's mercy for their own survival.

The process lined out in 18:15-20 carries with it the authority of heaven. Earlier in the gospel, we remember the crowds praising God for giving "such authority to human beings"(9:8). This is a great deal of authority to place in human hands and could easily be used as a weapon rather than as an instrument of mercy. Those who treat little ones well likely possess the character to bind and loose in ways that reflect the values of the kingdom of heaven.

❧ Reflection and Application

1. Why is a church's ministry to children important in developing a church's kingdom character? If a church treats children as second-class citizens, what will it lose?

2. How might the beatitudes help us define "little ones"? List characteristics of a church that would minister to children willingly and effectively. How does this list compare to the attributes found in the beatitudes?

1. Perhaps our sinful nature expresses itself most clearly in the business of forgiveness. Often, we would rather nurse our anger, eat rat poison, than reclaim our brother or sister. Nothing is more damaging to a church than unresolved conflict. My sense is that the process of reclaiming a brother or sister lined out in this chapter is most often short-circuited in the first step. We would rather gossip to others than go directly and privately to our brother or sister. Choose today to live mercifully. If you need to forgive or be forgiven, pray for the courage to go directly to your brother or sister.

2. Have you become too important in the church for children's ministry? You are drifting from the kingdom of heaven! Do something crazy. Commit to spending your time ministering to children.

10

LAST THINGS FIRST

MATTHEW 19:3-22:46

HUNGER AND THIRST

We hear a lot of discussion about family values these days. Most of the discussion focuses on the preservation of the "traditional family" – mom, dad, and kids. Lobbyists express concern that our culture's values no longer support, promote, or sustain this version of family.

How does Jesus define family in Matthew? Families of the New Testament world bear only passing resemblance to ours today. Even the most traditional families in our culture do not resemble the extended families found in the Bible or approximate the clearly divided worlds inhabited by men and women, masters and slaves, and parents and children. Beyond these differences, one would be hard pressed to hear a lobbyist say what Jesus says in Matthew 10, "I have come to set a man against his father, and a daughter against her mother,... and one's foes will be members of one's own household" (10:35-36). Jesus comes with a new definition of family that broke the bonds of the traditional family of his day (cf. 12:46-50). What kind of values support, promote, or sustain kingdom families? In this section, family values kingdom-style are on full display: *the first will be last, and the last will be first.*

HEARING THE TEXT

In previous lessons we have learned a number of things that enhance our reading and understanding. Many of the things we have learned about reading a gospel are present in this section. We have accounts unique to Matthew's gospel (19:10-12; 20:1-16; 21:28-32), minor differences in common stories (19:9-10, 21; 20:34; 21:14-15, 43; 22:11-14), editorial asides and summaries from the narrator (20:34; 22:46), and repeating themes or motifs (authority, compassion, perfection, fulfillment). As you read this section, notice how many insights you are gathering by paying careful attention to the way the story is told.

✿ Reflection and Application

Does this section have an overriding theme? What words or phrases seem to run throughout the section? Are there multiple threads in this section? If so, which seem to be major, which play a minor role?

HE MADE THEM MALE AND FEMALE

"Is it lawful to divorce one's wife *for any cause?*" The Pharisees' question draws Jesus into a debate already well under way in Jewish circles. Different schools of thought existed with regard to interpreting Deuteronomy 24:1-4. Followers of the rabbi Hillel taught that a wife could be divorced if her husband found her displeasing in any way. In contrast, the rabbi Shammai taught that the law permitted divorce only in the case of sexual impropriety on the part of the woman. It would appear that Jesus sides with Shammai when he says, "whoever divorces his wife, except for unchastity, and marries another commits adultery" (19:9).

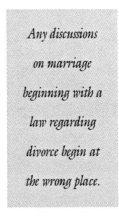

Any discussions on marriage beginning with a law regarding divorce begin at the wrong place.

Let's look closer, however, at Jesus' argument in Matthew and remember other pictures we have already seen. He begins with the positive statement of the place of marriage in God's eyes found in the creation story. God made humans male and female, and for this reason a man shall leave his father and mother and become one flesh with his wife. Any discussions on marriage beginning with a law regarding divorce begin at the wrong place. From the beginning God desired marriage to be permanent. In essence Jesus teaches, "Quit focusing on divorce, and focus on marriage in the will of God!"

Both Hillel and Shammai start with faulty foundations. They see divorce as a male prerogative. The law assumed that only husbands could initiate divorce. Jesus sees marriage, however, not from the husband's perspective, but from God's. This means Jesus begins with the reality that male and female together are created in the image of God. Women are not merely disposable property created to please men. They are co-bearers of God's likeness. As one flesh, husband and wife represent God in a unique way that should not be altered.

Why then did Moses allow for a certificate of divorce? "It was because you were so hard-hearted," Jesus responds. Divorce is a concession to the sinful nature. Here again we see a principle important to Jesus throughout Matthew's gospel. There is something greater than the letter of the law. Behind the law stands God's heart. Behind the law stands the face of one's neighbor, whether male or female, created in the image of God. In this case, as with others, it is possible to keep the law and not do the will of God. Jesus' teaching on marriage in Matthew 19 is a call to a deeper righteousness, a righteousness that exceeds that of Hillel or Shammai. Jesus calls his listeners to imitate the heart of God, and in this way to be perfect as God is perfect.

The disciples are astounded by Jesus' demanding view of marriage. "It is better not to marry," they conclude. Who would decide to marry under these demanding conditions? Joseph would. Jesus' teaching here reminds us of the opening story in which Joseph decides not to divorce Mary, but to take her as his wife. Like the Pharisees, Joseph's first response to Mary's circumstance is to review his options for divorce according to the law. God moves Joseph beyond the law to embrace marriage, even in a difficult circumstance. Joseph's decision for marriage is now based on mercy, a value close to God's heart, instead of his rights as a husband pertaining to divorce. He models, for Matthew's church and ours, a higher righteousness.

⅜ Reflection and Application

The focus of this text is clearly on God's will and design for marriage. Has this been our focus as we have studied the text? Has our focus on this text been in the right place? What would we gain by returning our focus to Jesus' view of marriage instead of what constitutes a "scriptural divorce?"

THE LAST SHALL BE FIRST

Jesus views family here from the perspective of those least valued from a cultural perspective. In the discussion on marriage and divorce, a discussion in which the Pharisees assume that only husbands have rights, Jesus recovers a place for women as co-bearers of the image of God. He exalts the lowly member in the discussion. The same is true with the discussion on eunuchs. Jesus suggests that for the sake of the kingdom, some might actually choose to be eunuchs, the reference here being figurative and not literal. Jesus holds open the option of singleness in the new family of God. While this might not seem out of place to us, singleness was simply not an option for most in Jesus' day. Single people stood out and were often seen as deviants. But in the new family of God, the last are first, and eunuchs have a valued place. The picture of family is complete with Jesus' welcoming of the children. In Jesus' day, children were to be seen and not heard, and not seen all that often. Yet, Jesus welcomes them and blesses them. The last shall be first. These are family values in the kingdom of heaven.

What is implicit in the description of marriage, singleness, and children, becomes explicit in the next three stories. The disciples, who refuse to let children come to Jesus, express astonishment when the rich young man is sent away grieving. "Who then can be saved?" they ask incredulously (19:25). Jesus answers that those who leave everything for the kingdom of heaven will inherit a hundredfold when the kingdom is realized. Some who are first will be last, and the last will be first. Matthew joins to the story of the rich young man the parable of the laborers in the vineyard, a parable unique to Matthew (20:1-16). Here, those workers who began labor late in the day receive the same wages as those who began in the early morning. Those who came first are naturally resentful and do not recognize the graciousness of the owner of the vineyard. Again, the last will be first and the first will be last. Finally, the third prediction of Jesus' death and resurrection is followed by the request of the mother of James and John for places of prominence for her sons in Jesus' kingdom (20:20-28). This request demonstrates a lack of awareness of how power works in the kingdom. Power is expressed in submission, "and whoever wishes to be first among you must be your slave; just as the Son of Man came not to be served but to give his life as a ransom for many" (20:27-28).

✺ Reflection and Application

We hear more and more in our churches about the importance of strengthening families. An unintended result of this emphasis is that single persons sometimes feel insignificant, or like second-class citizens. How would Jesus' teaching in this section alter our perspectives on the place and role of single people in the family of God?

NO ONE DARED ASK HIM ANY MORE QUESTIONS

Jesus' dramatic entrance into Jerusalem incites a series of conflicts concerning the nature of Jesus' authority. Jesus answers the challenge of the religious leaders with parables of judgement (21:28-22:14). The kingdom is being taken from the original tenants (represented by the scribes and Pharisees), and given to others who honor God's servant, even prostitutes and tax-collectors. Jesus demonstrates a greater grasp of the law than the religious teachers by answering questions about taxes, the resurrection, and the greatest commandment, and by posing questions no one else can answer (22:15-46). He is the authoritative teacher of Israel.

These controversies stand against the backdrop of Jesus' purification of the temple (21:12-27). The temple stood for ages as a sign of God's presence among his people. His glory dwells in Zion. Yet, what Jesus finds is a temple that no longer glorifies God or signifies his presence. It is a den of robbers, not a house of prayer. In contrast to the practice of the money changers, Jesus represents God's presence by healing the blind and the lame. God's presence expressed in the healing ministry of Jesus naturally calls forth praise. The innocent and uninhibited praise of children (21:15-17) stands in contrast to the grumbling and complaining of the chief priests and the elders (21:23). We are reminded again that the last will be first and the first will be last.

A Closer Look

1. In our culture divorce is an epidemic. As Christians, we want to make commitments to strengthen marriages. Four realities stand behind the strong view of marriage presented in Matthew. First, our spouse is created in the image of God and exists for his glory, not our own. Second, the value of mercy is greater than any cause for divorce. Every divorce, even a "scriptural one," is a concession to hardness of heart and a negation of the greater standard of mercy. Third, just as Joseph took Mary as his wife on the condition of God's continuing presence, so we know and affirm that there is no hardship we can face as married people that moves us away from the empowering presence of God. Finally, kingdom marriages are built on the values of the cross, the first will be last and the last will be

59

first. Using these teachings from Matthew, take inventory of your marriage and commit yourselves to the higher righteousness of the kingdom.

2. Having made these strong statements concerning marriage, I also want to reaffirm the merciful standard for Jesus' understanding of family in Matthew. Single people, including those who have suffered the tragedy of divorce, are no less entitled to mercy than members of "traditional families." Pray that God will give your church a "last will be first" heart so that all members might know the family values of the kingdom.

11

THE ONE WHO ENDURES WILL BE SAVED

MATTHEW 23:1-25:46

HUNGER AND THIRST

We are not a very patient people. We expect results, and results now. This is as true of our spiritual expectations as it is of auto repairs or business dealings. We want five simple steps to an overcoming spiritual life. We do not wait well. We have lost the capacity to be watchful and disciplined. As a result, we see God only in the triumphant moment and miss his presence in the long, dark journey. We think of the spiritual life as a series of sprints, short dashes, and bursts of brilliance. Jesus, in Matthew's gospel, sees spirituality as an endurance event. This is important for Matthew's church to remember since their stage in the race is difficult and slow. Still, Jesus urges, "I am with you, be watchful." This spirituality develops a different set of muscles, muscles we are unaccustomed to flexing in our results-oriented culture. These are muscles we will need to endure to the end.

> We have lost the capacity to be watchful and disciplined. As a result, we see God only in the triumphant moment and miss his presence in the long, dark journey.

HEARING THE STORY

This is the final of the five discourses in Matthew. As you read, notice again the correspondences between the Sermon on the Mount and these important chapters. While the Sermon on the Mount is a positive statement of the kingdom agenda of Jesus, this final section provides a negative portrayal of values opposite to the kingdom. As you read, see if you can make a list of contrasting statements from Matthew. For example, "Come to me, all you who are weary and heavy-burdened..." (11:28), and "They tie up heavy burdens....but are unwilling to lift a finger to help bear them" (23:4).

✢ Reflection and Application

What adjectives would you use to describe the tone of this final teaching section in Matthew? What purpose would ending with this tone serve? How would Matthew's church have responded to this section?

CALL NO ONE ON EARTH YOUR FATHER

Like a graceful dance partner, the final discourse in Matthew's gospel inversely traces the steps of the Sermon on the Mount. In the Sermon on the Mount, Jesus suggests that those who will be called great in the kingdom of heaven teach *and* observe the commandments of God (5:19). These possess a righteousness exceeding that of the scribes and Pharisees. In step with the Sermon on the Mount, the final discourse warns of scribes and Pharisees who teach the commandments of God but do not keep them. Though they occupy Moses' seat, a place of authority in the synagogue communities, they are not faithful teachers. Unlike Jesus, whose yoke is easy and burden light, the scribes and Pharisees tie on heavy burdens and are unwilling to lift a finger to help bear them. Unlike the pious in the kingdom of heaven who do their good deeds in secret, the scribes and Pharisees "do all their deeds to be seen by others" (23:5). Broad phylacteries, long fringes, honored seats in the synagogues, and titles of honor are all indicators of a surface righteousness subject to the charge of hypocrisy.

The negative descriptions of the scribes and Pharisees in the opening verses of the final discourse provide fascinating insight into Matthew's understanding of Christian community. Followers of Jesus recognize only the authority of heaven. They reserve the titles "rabbi," "Father," and "instructor" for God and his Messiah. While Matthew's gospel allows a role for Christian scribes and prophets, their authority is always derived from the authority of the risen Jesus who continues to be "with them." Instead of wearing titles of distinction, followers of Jesus carry the designations "brother" or "servant."

Matthew's church gathers under the authority of heaven without any member being able to claim privileged positions. To use language familiar to our tradition, they live as "brethren." The church envisioned by Jesus stands in contrast to the synagogue communities of Matthew's day who increasingly used the designation of "Rabbi" to honor authoritative teachers. Rabbis, in turn, "instructed" or "mastered" followers who someday might achieve the more honored status of Rabbi.

The language of Jesus in Matthew counters this vision of making disciples at every turn. Jesus' followers are always disciples, and the position of a disciple is not some preliminary stage to becoming something greater, like a rabbi. Moreover, Jesus refuses the title of rabbi for himself. Only God is Rabbi. In light of this, it is interesting to note that unlike the other gospels, only one follower of Jesus in Matthew's gospel refers to him as "Rabbi." In contrast to Peter who confesses Jesus properly (16:16), the betrayer, Judas, calls Jesus "Rabbi" in the dramatic scene at the Last Supper (26:25).

Unlike the synagogues where authority is invested in "Moses' seat," the church that follows Jesus resists authoritarian models of leadership. Instead, the authority of

Jesus is worked out in a community of relative equals who call each other brother and sister and understand themselves only as servants.

✨ Reflection and Application

From what you have seen in this text and throughout the gospel, how would you describe community from Jesus' perspective in Matthew? Is it hierarchical? Is it a community of equals? Who are its leaders? How do they function? Who makes the decisions? What are the implications of eliminating titles of honor and calling one another simply "brother" or "sister"? How do you think power would be understood and exercised? What can we learn from Matthew's portrait of community?

JUSTICE, MERCY, AND FAITH

Matthew's readers have no need for a scorecard to determine the identity of the players. "Woe to you, scribes and Pharisees, hypocrites!" This blistering denunciation clearly marks out the "bad guys" in Matthew's gospel. The "woes" remind us that Jesus' teaching began with beatitudes in the opening lines of the Sermon on the Mount. The attentive reader is not surprised to find in the woes themes found in the Sermon on the Mount and other strategic places in the gospel. Here again we find words about hypocrites, persecuted prophets, oath taking, binding and loosing, and being clean on the inside. While comments could be made about each of the woes, two themes command our attention at this point.

The second woe (23:15) castigates the scribes and Pharisees for their missionary zeal. With very strong language Jesus condemns their practice, "You cross sea and land to make a single convert, and you make the new convert twice as much a child of hell as yourselves." Woe, indeed! These words are striking when heard in relation to the Great Commission at the end of the gospel, "Go . . . and make disciples" (28:19). Clearly, Christian disciple making should distinguish itself from that of the scribes and the Pharisees. Remember the first Great Commission we noticed in Matthew's gospel addressed specifically to the Pharisees, "Go and learn what this means, 'I desire mercy, not sacrifice'" (9:13). I would suggest that Jesus has no interest in anyone crossing land and sea to make disciples in his name unless they know first the difference between the ways of mercy and sacrifice.

This brings us to our second theme prominent in the woes. We noticed earlier that the middle beatitude features mercy. "Blessed are the merciful, for they shall receive mercy" (5:7). In rhythm with the beatitudes, the middle woe stresses the importance of mercy over sacrifice (23:23-24). The Pharisees, demonstrating the way of sacrifice, keep the letter of the law to avoid the demanding heart of the law. They tithe their spices but neglect the weightier matters of the law: justice, mercy, and faith. Notice that Jesus upholds all of the law: "these you ought to have practiced without neglecting the others." He came not to abolish the law, but to fulfill it. However, we

63

also see again that Jesus faithfully interprets the law because he knows its heart, its intent. He knows what weighs the most, and therefore can bind and loose according to the interests of the kingdom of heaven. Given what we have seen to this point, it is not surprising that we should find mercy front and center.

✿ Reflection and Application

1. If your church used Matthew's gospel as a measure for mission-readiness, how would you fare? What kind of questions might Jesus ask your elders, your ministers, and members before exhorting them to go into the world making disciples? Have you seen evangelistic activity that is not in keeping with the concerns of Jesus in Matthew? Can evangelism be unmerciful? What would that look like?

2. Not many in our churches tithe their mint, dill, and cumin, but are we ever guilty of emphasizing some things over weightier matters like justice, mercy, and faith? What can we learn from 23:23-24 regarding the difference between the way of sacrifice and the way of mercy? At this point in the gospel, how would you define the way of sacrifice? How do we keep weightier matters at the forefront to avoid a mindset of sacrifice?

COME, YOU THAT ARE BLESSED BY MY FATHER

What is a desolating sacrilege (24:15)? Sounds like a skin condition. Why is Jesus talking about it, and what does it have to do with me? The last sections of the final discourse contain images and pictures very foreign to us. The section is full of what scholars refer to as apocalyptic imagery.[1] While there are a number of interpretations of apocalyptic literature, these types of sayings are always designed to encourage God's people living in difficult circumstances. This is certainly true of the apocalyptic passages in Matthew.

Apocalyptic literature is nearly always produced during times of great stress and persecution. The imaginative language of books like Daniel and Revelation suggest to those being oppressed that glorious times lie ahead. Oppressed people have a hard time believing they are on the winning side of history. Followers drop by the wayside if the cause appears to be a lost one. Apocalyptic perspectives encourage believers to look beyond history to a guaranteed, victorious outcome in the last days. This view helps persecuted people find courage for their convictions, and belief that their sufferings are a prelude to a final and glorious victory.

Matthew's church undoubtedly read Jesus' words in this section with great interest, hoping to find enough clues to suggest that their shabby circumstances were actually the prelude to eternal glory. The parables of the faithful servant (24:45-51), the wise bridesmaids (25:1-13), and the talents teach the virtues of perseverance,

---

[1] For further explanation of apocalyptic literature, see Ian Fair's study guide on Revelation in the Streams of Mercy Study Series, HillCrest Publishing, 2000.

watchfulness, and productivity to a people living in perilous and uncertain times. The message of this apocalyptic section is clear: "The one who endures to the end will be saved" (24:13).

Finally, this section offers a compelling picture of the final judgment. On that day, the Son of Man himself will separate the sheep from the goats. Some on that day will hear the greatest of all beatitudes, "Come, you that are blessed by my Father, inherit the kingdom prepared for you from the foundation of the world" (25:34). Who are these blessed ones? Those who showed mercy to the hungry, the stranger, the naked, and those in prison. The surprise of the judgment scene is that ministry to these "little ones" is also ministry to Jesus himself. He is "with them." Moreover, those deemed righteous on that final day not only ministered to Jesus, but to his church – "the least of these who are my brothers" (25:40). Blessed are the merciful, for they shall receive mercy.

🕯 Reflection and Application

1. Matthew's gospel promises that Jesus is with us, even to the end of the age. But if we wanted to find Jesus to be with him, where would we look? What are Jesus' concerns in the final judgment?

2. If apocalyptic imagery is designed to provide encouragement for beleagured people, what kinds of encouragement does this section offer? What encouragement do you and your church need to be ready for the coming of the Son of Man?

A Closer Look

1. This section clearly calls disciples to watchfulness. While the Son of Man will come at an unexpected hour (24:44), Christians must be found ready. How does one stay ready? The final phrase of the Lord's Prayer is translated by the NRSV, "And do not bring us to the time of trial, but rescue us from the evil one" (6:13). The "time of trial" most likely refers to a scene like the one in Matthew 25:31-46. Those who pray in this way hope to be spared the negative judgment of God. For this to happen they need protection from the evil one. Find again the discipline of saying the Lord's Prayer and meditate on the final phrase.

2. Those who do not look for Jesus in this age are not likely to recognize him when he comes in the age to come. We recognize Jesus most clearly in the faces of the "little ones," the stranger, the naked, the hungry, the orphan, the prisoner. Make sure you look for Jesus this week. Choose to be with him as he has chosen to be with you.

12

POURED OUT FOR THE
FORGIVENESS OF SINS

MATTHEW 26:1-27:61

HUNGER AND THIRST

I once baptized a young woman who struggled for nearly a year to make some sense of the death of Jesus. She wanted badly to be a Christian, but could not come to grips with the pain and tragedy precisely at the center of the gospel story. Why did Jesus have to die? Was there no other way for God to reconcile his people to himself?

She was asking the most important question in considering Christianity. What does one do with the death of Jesus? The amount of space given to the death of Jesus in Matthew suggests that this is an important question for understanding the gospel.

> She wanted the experience of dying with Christ to drench her for as long as possible, even if that meant drip drying.

The young woman I baptized did come to grips eventually with the importance of the cross. The day she was baptized she carried her grandmother's silver cross into the baptistry with her. After she was baptized, she refused towels from the helpful ladies waiting to receive their new sister. She wanted the experience of dying with Christ to drench her for as long as possible, even if that meant drip drying. Reading this story again allows us to ask anew what it means to be baptized into the one who suffered and died for us.

HEARING THE TEXT

All roads in Matthew lead to these culminating chapters. Through the use of foreshadowing and prediction, Matthew brings the reader through the gospel to its inescapable climax: the death of Jesus. In these thickly-textured narratives, Matthew brings various threads together to depict a compelling picture of the saving significance of Jesus' death. This is the dramatic high-point of the story.

The reader participates in this drama through the striking character portraits provided by Matthew's account. As Carroll and Green point out,

> The characters in the drama...enact for the reader sharply divergent responses to issues of life and death that overtake them. In this parade of

characters are glimpsed models of trust and fidelity, of loyalty and courage. Yet alongside them, one cannot miss their sometimes horrible, sometimes tragic counterparts, paradigms of treachery and cowardice, of infidelity and coercive power. That is, Matthew confronts the reader with fundamental issues of human character and purpose when he brings the characters of his story face-to-face with the death of the Messiah.[1]

Let these characters bring you face-to-face with the death of the Messiah as you read these crucial texts.

❧ Reflection and Application

As you read the narratives in this section, make two lists of characters in your mind. Who are those who display loyalty and courage? Who are those who display cowardice, treachery, or infidelity? What do you make of the two lists?

IN MEMORY OF HER

Three characters figure prominently in the stories leading up to Jesus' death: the woman who anoints Jesus, Judas, and Peter. It is not surprising to find Peter playing a prominent role. Peter's behavior here is consistent with what we have seen of him before. He believes and confesses that Jesus is the Christ, the Son of God, *but* protests Jesus' prediction of his death. Peter, in faith, steps out onto the water to walk with Jesus, *but* loses faith and sinks. Here again, Peter expresses his desire to be a model follower of Jesus, even to death. "Though all become deserters because of you, I will never desert you" (26:33). Surely, we want to say the same thing! Our hearts are crushed with Peter, however, as Jesus' prediction of his betrayal comes to pass. As the cock crows we too know the weakness of the human heart, the failure of true intentions, and so weep with Peter. Again he sinks into the water of little faith.

Peter's failure heightens our sense of Jesus' solitude as he faced death. Peter follows, though only at a distance, while the other disciples have already fled. Strike the shepherd, scatter the sheep. Matthew reports, "all the disciples deserted him and fled" (26:56). The failure of the eleven is exceeded only by the betrayal by Judas. While Peter shows authentic faith with wavering loyalty, Judas represents counterfeit faith. The reader is not surprised by Judas' betrayal of Jesus. Even early in the gospel, he is the "one who betrayed Jesus" (10:4). The betrayal is bitter. It comes from one who has shared bread, "dipped his hand into the bowl," with Jesus. It comes from one who betrays him with a kiss. Many have speculated concerning Judas' motives. Matthew provides only one: thirty pieces of silver.

The most impressive portrait of faithfulness to Jesus comes from a surprising

---

[1] John.T. Carroll and Joel Marcus Green, *The Death of Jesus in Early Christianity*, (Peabody, MA: Henderickson, 1995), 39.

source. This disciple is not one of the twelve. This disciple is an unnamed woman. She appears only here. We know precious few details about her. Yet, Jesus says of her that "wherever this good news is proclaimed in the whole world, what she has done will be told in memory of her" (26:13). What has she done? She has demonstrated love for Jesus by anointing his feet with expensive ointment. Combined in this event are expressions of joy, luxury, honor, divine approval, and consecration. Indeed, she has honored and recognized Jesus' place before God by anointing his body for burial. Like Samuel pouring oil on the head of David, this woman has marked out God's anointed for his divinely ordained mission. In effect, she blesses him for his willingness to be obedient to death, even death on a cross. She stands in contrast to the disciples who complain about the extravagance of the gift. Her expensive gift also stands in contrast to Judas who betrayed Jesus for thirty pieces of silver. Jesus expects that disciples will live, not only in memory of him, but also in memory of her.

❧ Reflection and Application

Notice the portrait of women in the scenes surrounding Jesus' death. Finding a place of prominence with the anonymous woman who anoints Jesus are the women from Galilee who follow Jesus all the way to the cross (27:55-56). How do they compare to the twelve? Notice even Pilate's wife who proclaims Jesus' innocence in the midst of the trials (27:19). The positive examples of faith in these difficult scenes belong almost exclusively to women. Why is the memory of this important? Do we tell the story of the women in this scenes? What do we lose by forgetting them? How would we be changed if we remembered them?

THIS IS MY BLOOD, POURED OUT FOR MANY

What is the meaning of Jesus' death? This might be the most important question of Christian theology. Matthew pursues it by focusing on the theme of shed blood. For instance, Judas' truthful recognition is that he has "sinned in betraying innocent blood" (27:4). Judas throws down the money at the feet of the chief priests and elders who recognize it as "blood money" (vs. 6). Instead of donating the money to the temple treasury, they buy a potter's field for the burial of Judas, a field "called the Field of Blood to this day" (vs. 10).

The theme of innocent blood is picked up again with Pilate in material unique to Matthew. Pilate washes his hands before the crowd, declaring "I am innocent of this man's blood, see to it yourself" (27:24). The lynching crowd replies, "His blood be on us and our children" (vs. 25). Human actors share blame for shedding the blood of the innocent Jesus.

Despite others' guilt in shedding Jesus' blood, his death is also portrayed positively as the work of God. Jesus' innocent suffering ties him to the tradition of the prophets, a prominent theme in Matthew. Remember, the final two beatitudes have to do with suffering for righteousness' sake (5:10-12). The corresponding final woe in chapter 23 denounces the scribes and the Pharisees for partnership with those who persecuted and killed the prophets "in the days of our ancestors." Jesus describes the plight of the church, "Therefore, I send you prophets, sages, and scribes, some of whom you will kill and crucify... so that upon you may come all the righteous blood shed on earth, from the blood of the righteous Abel to the blood of Zechariah..." (vss. 29-36). The blood of Jesus unites the suffering of all the people of God throughout history. His resurrection vindicates their innocence.

This theme of vindication is not the only positive interpretation of the blood of Jesus in Matthew. In Matthew, Mark, and Luke, Jesus describes the cup at the Last Supper as "my blood of the covenant." Only Matthew, however, adds "which is poured out for many for the forgiveness of sins" (26:28-29). Jesus' death is the offering of an innocent sacrifice for the forgiveness of sins. No longer will God's people look to temple sacrifices for their forgiveness. They now will look to Jesus.

✺ Reflection and Application

Before Jesus offered his life as a sacrifice for sin, God's people looked to the temple and its altar as the primary place for worship. For Christians, the altar has been replaced with a table where Jesus offers his body and blood to maintain covenant with his people. What difference does it make to see a table, not an altar, as the primary place for Christian worship? How do we experience the forgiveness of Jesus around the table? How does that forgiveness impact the way we see our brothers and sisters gathered with us around Jesus' table?

LET GOD DELIVER HIM NOW

Some pictures leave more lasting impressions than others. The picture of Jesus praying in the garden impressed other New Testament writers. For example, the writer of Hebrews remembers that Jesus "while in the flesh, offered up prayers and supplications, with loud cries and tears, to the one who was able to save him from death" (Heb 5:7). We are very familiar with the words of Jesus' prayer, "My Father, if it is possible, let this cup pass from me" (26:39). In the garden, in agony, he prays for reprieve while his disciples sleep. He prays alone. He dies alone. His agonizing prayer in the garden is joined by his cry from the cross, "My God, my God, why have you forsaken me?" (27.46).

Jesus' death is his choice, an act of obedience.

The chief priests, scribes, and elders derisively call upon Jesus to use his power to end the ordeal of his death. "You who would destroy the temple and rebuild it in three days, save yourself!" They mock him, "he saved others, he cannot save himself." The reader knows, however, that Jesus can save himself. Satan too knew this when he invited Jesus to throw himself from the pinnacle of the temple, allowing God's angels to catch him (4:6). Jesus' death is his choice, an act of obedience. The religious leaders rightly confess Jesus even as they doubt his connection to the Father, "He trusts in God, let God deliver him now" (27:40-43). Jesus does trust God, even through the agony of death on a cross. The writer of Hebrews suggests that God heard Jesus' cries precisely because of his "reverent submission. Although he was a Son, he learned obedience through what he suffered; and having been made perfect, he became the source of eternal salvation for all who obey him" (5:7-9). On the cross we not only see Jesus as a sacrifice for sin, but as a model of trusting obedience. We see at the cross the loving character of God.

❧ Reflection and Application

What picture of Jesus do you gain from Matthew's account of his death? What traits do you find in him that draw you closer? What would it mean to follow someone who gave himself this way?

A CLOSER LOOK

1. Jesus poured himself out for the forgiveness of sins. After viewing the lonely, agonizing death of Jesus, who could take sin lightly? The foot of the cross is an appropriate place to confess sin and receive the forgiveness of God. You may need a trustworthy brother or sister to hear your confession and speak over you the forgiveness of God. Remember, when two or three of you are gathered to bind and loose, Jesus is there with you.

2. Jesus shows us in his death what it means to be God's person. He trusts God completely even in the face of death. He is obedient to God's will even when it seems contrary to his self-interests. Season your prayers this week with the words of Jesus, "Not my will, but yours be done." By praying this way, entrust your life to God.

13

I AM WITH YOU ALWAYS, TO THE END OF THE AGE

MATTHEW 27:57-28:20

HUNGER AND THIRST

We love perfect endings. As a sports fan I like a certain poetry to the end of a successful career. Michael Jordan walked away from basketball moments after sinking the winning jump shot in a championship game. Ted Williams hit a home run in his final at bat. John Elway walked away a Super Bowl champion. These endings fittingly represent and express brilliant careers.

The same is true of the last scene in Matthew's gospel. The Great Commission leaves us with a compelling and victorious final picture of Jesus. More than this, however, his final words tie together in a memorable fashion the major themes and motifs of the gospel. These oft-memorized verses hold a place of honor in most of our churches. My sense is that they were often repeated in Matthew's church as well. My prayer is that as they are read at the conclusion of this study, they will be filled with all the meanings and resonances of this magnificent gospel. As we say them over again, we will join the voices of those who read them first and will be enriched by this enlarged fellowship.

HEARING THE STORY

The resurrection appearances of Jesus occupy very little space in Matthew. We move quickly from an empty tomb to an ascending Jesus. Missing are many of the accounts of Jesus' dealings with fallen followers and doubting disciples. The brevity of this account certainly leaves us with different impressions than, for instance, Luke's extensive accounts. As you read, form a sense of the dramatic effect of the ending of this gospel. Sometimes brevity communicates in ways that more expanded narratives cannot. What is Matthew doing here?

✢ Reflection and Application

1. While Matthew's resurrection account is shorter than others, it is almost completely unique. Notice, for instance, 27:62-66, 28:11-15. Why would these reports be especially important to Matthew? What have we seen previously that prepares us to understand the significance of this account? How might these accounts help us understand the background for the writing of Matthew's gospel?

2. What is the dramatic effect of the brevity of this account? With what images are you left? Is your eye drawn several places, or just one? What adjectives would you use to describe the effect of this ending?

THEY TOOK HOLD OF HIS FEET AND WORSHIPPED HIM

Every Sunday followers of Jesus gather for worship, bringing with them joys, fears, beliefs, and doubts. They find good company in the closing episodes of Matthew's gospel. Mary Magdalene and "the other Mary" hear the angel's announcement concerning Jesus' resurrection and run from the tomb with both fear and joy (28:1-8). Even the magnificent scene of Jesus' ascension into heaven is met with both worshipful belief and doubt on the part of the disciples (28:17). The picture of disciples in Matthew is mixed. Those who follow Jesus demonstrate both faith and fear. Inconsistency, however, does not disqualify one from worshipping the risen Lord. Throughout Matthew, Jesus' ministry has called forth worship and adoration (2:2; 9:8; 14:33). Even in our inconsistency we are called to join the women in laying hold of Jesus' feet and worshipping him.

The worshipful response of Jesus' followers stands in contrast to the scheming and self-calculation of the chief priests and Pharisees. Only Matthew reports the extra efforts of the religious leaders to fortify the tomb where Jesus is buried. Only here do we hear of lies and rumors spread "among the Jews to this day" (27:62-66; 28:11-15). Undoubtedly, these stories reflect the tension between Matthew's church and the synagogues. These stories of scheming and self-calculation also bring the story full-circle. As with the news of Jesus' birth, his resurrection brings forth two telling responses. Just as Joseph did, the fearful women at the empty tomb do what the angel commands, and, just like the Magi, these women pay homage to Jesus. However, the fear and subsequent scheming of Herod is also reproduced in the dealings of the chief priests and Pharisees. The story ends as it begins, leaving us to cast our lot with models of trusting faith and worship, or with calculating unbelief.

✌ Reflection and Application

Churches these days spend a lot of time discussing worship renewal. What might Matthew contribute to our conversation? What images of worship do we see in this gospel? What is the cause for worship in Matthew? Can we have worship renewal apart from an encounter with the risen Jesus?

ALL AUTHORITY IN HEAVEN AND ON EARTH

Jesus taught his followers to pray, "on earth as it is in heaven." This prayer can be offered in Jesus' name since all authority in heaven and on earth belong to the risen one. Matthew portrays Jesus' authority persistently from beginning to end of this gospel. He is the Davidic ruler who is to "shepherd my people Israel" (2:6). His teaching is not like the scribes and Pharisees, but comes with authority, even an authority to move beyond the law (7:29). His acts of healing demonstrate his authority over nature, disease, and sin so that the crowds marvel, glorifying God for giving such authority to humans (9:8). Indeed, authority is given to humans. Jesus grants authority to Peter to unlock the gates of heaven (16:19), and he grants authority to the church to bind and loose (18:18). In the name of Jesus the church bears the awesome authority of the risen one to make it in heaven as it is on earth through binding and loosing. The final conflicts with the scribes and Pharisees demonstrate again Jesus' authority in relation to the law. Though Matthew's churches may be suffering the pains of separation from the synagogue community, they can chart their own way independently and confidently under the all encompassing authority of the one they call "Lord."

At the beginning of the gospel Jesus calls disciples to become fishers of people. His final words send them into the world to do just that. Jesus' authority is to be spent making disciples. These words call to mind both Jesus' early commission to the Pharisees, "go and learn... 'mercy, not sacrifice'"(9:13), and his condemnation of the Pharisees for making disciples for hell (23:15). Jesus' followers are not to make just any kind of follower. They are to teach others to observe all that Jesus commanded. With the entire sweep of Matthew's story in full view, Jesus' commands find their center in the practice of mercy. This is good for our churches to hear. Too often, we hear only the word "baptize" when we read the Great Commission. Baptism is certainly a necessary aspect of making disciples. But the goal is to make disciples of Jesus. We are to baptize people into a particular way of life – the way of mercy over sacrifice. We might do better than asking of our missionaries or our churches, "how many baptisms have you had?" A better question might be, "how many merciful disciples are being made?"

✣ Reflection and Application

1. How did you understand the Great Commission before our study of Matthew? How have your perceptions changed given a careful reading of the entire gospel? What changes in your church would bring you more into line with this great commission from Jesus?

2. Do we have even the faintest idea what it means for Jesus to have all authority in heaven and on earth? More astounding is the permission Jesus gives his church to carry out kingdom business in his name. How would our experience of the kingdom change if we became more conscious of the power and authority given to the church? Would we be more bold or humble? This is a lot of authority to give fragile people. How should our awareness of this authority influence the type of leaders we choose?

I AM WITH YOU ALWAYS

Matthew's gospel whispers a persistent theme in the ear of the reader. Though Mary's pregnancy opens your life to shame, Joseph, I am with you. Though Herod seeks to kill all the male children, I am with you. Though you are sent out like sheep in the midst of the wolves, I am with you. Though you are dragged before councils and flogged in synagogues, I am with you. When you bind and loose, I am with you. Though I go into the heavens, I am not going away. As I send you among the nations to make disciples, I am with you. Always. Always. Even to the end of the age. The one who endures to the end will be saved. Those who endure will learn to call him Emmanuel – God with us.

Words like those from a hymn we sing may very well have been close to the hearts of Matthew's church as well.

Be with me Lord, I cannot live without Thee, I dare not try to take one step alone, I cannot bear the loads of life unaided, I need thy strength to lean myself upon.

Be with me Lord, no other gift or blessing thou could'st bestow could with this one compare –

A constant sense of they abiding presence, Where-e'er I am, to feel that thou art near. [1]

These are important sentiments for a church in the throes of transition. Matthew's church was in the midst of learning a new way of life—a way that valued both things old and things new. This sounds very familiar as I reflect on the context of our churches. In an age of rapid and massive cultural and social change, the church finds itself constantly evaluating things both old and new. It is reassuring to hear the promise of God to a church in transition. I am with you always, to the end of the age.

While our pressures might be different than those of the first readers of Matthew's gospel, we all experience the difficulties of this life. Each Sunday the church gathers to lay hold of the feet of Jesus, bringing the weight of life's cares with us. "Come to me," Jesus beckons. "I will give you rest." I believe Matthew, a scribe trained for the kingdom of heaven, at the conclusion of the reading of this gospel would lift his hands to speak a blessing over the gathering of the church – God's little ones. "Remember, our Lord says, 'I am with you always, to the end of the age.'" Praise you, Emmanuel!

✸ Reflection and Application

1. How many times have you seen yourself or your church in the pages of this gospel? What stories from Matthew seem familiar to you? Has reading this gospel allowed you to experience more fully the presence of God? Do you know Jesus more fully as Emmanuel—God with us?

---

[1] T.O. Chisholm, "Be With Me, Lord," Copyright, 1963, L.O. Sanderson.

2. How does the promise of God's continuing presence at the end of this gospel effect the way you see your discipleship? If you truly believed the promise, how might you live differently?

A Closer Look

1. Make a list of three prominent ideas or sayings of Jesus that you think are central to this gospel. Find a prominent place to put them – in your Bible, on your refrigerator, your bathroom mirror. Let them serve as reminders in the next few weeks of the journey we have made through this gospel. Let them lead you to prayer. Let them remind you of God's continuing presence.

2. Two pictures form the heart of discipleship in Matthew. First, we must have a depth of righteousness that exceeds that of the scribes and Pharisees. Second, we must be committed to the way of mercy. Make a commitment to deepen your discipleship in both of these aspects. You might want to form a group of two or three who will gather for prayer and sharing. What better way to respond to Matthew's gospel than to form a group that would bind each member to a higher righteousness while simultaneously extending to one another the mercy of God!